Getting
Your
Own Way

Getting Your Own Way

A GUIDE TO GROWING UP ASSERTIVELY

Mary E. Mihaly

M Evans
Lanham • New York • Boulder • Toronto • Plymouth, UK

The chart on page 106 was developed by Dr. Joseph Zinker and his colleagues at The Gestalt Institute of Cleveland, Ohio in 1976. Reprinted by permission of Dr. Zinker. For further information consult *Creative Process in Gestalt Therapy* (New York: Brunner/Mazel, Inc.).

Specified material on pages 160-161 from *Motivation and Personality,* 2nd Edition, by Abraham H. Maslow. Copyright © 1970 by Abraham H. Maslow. By permission of Harper & Row, Publisher, Inc.

Library of Congress Cataloging in Publication Data

Mihaly, Mary, E.
    Getting your own way, A guide to growing
        up assertively.

    SUMMARY: Discusses assertive techniques that teenagers can use to protect themselves from feeling pushed around by parents, teachers, and peers.
        1. Youth—Juvenile literature.   2. Adolescence—Juvenile literature.   3. Assertiveness (Psychology)—Juvenile literature.   4. Adolescent psychology—Juvenile literature.   5. Interpersonal relations—Juvenile literature.   [1. Assertiveness (Psychology) 2. Interpersonal relations]   I. Title.

HQ796.M475   1979   301.43'15   78-27050
ISBN 978-1-59077-306-2

M Evans
An imprint of Rowman & Littlefield
4501 Forbes Boulevard, Suite 200
Lanham, Maryland 20706
www.rowman.com

Design by RFS Graphic Design, Inc.

Manufactured in the United States of America

Distributed by National Book Network

To my parents, George and Eva Mihaly, who gave their children space, and of whom I am immensely proud

CONTENTS

Writing a book seems an exotic thing to do, until one sits down to do it. The following individuals allowed me to share that reality with them, not always under the most convenient circumstances. Each had something to do with the completion of this book, and their contributions are recognized here with my deepest personal thanks.

My tribe—Mom and Dad, Carol and Merle, George and Lana, Margie, Joy, Mike, Matthew, Benjamin, and Aunt Mary—give my life richness. For their love and support, I am' grateful.

A few friends' kindness and encouragement set them apart: Patrick and Mike, who accept everything; Ronda, who let me kidnap her typewriter; Barb, who brings eggs and warmth to my kitchen; Chet, whose loyalty is as uncompromised as his poetry; Margaret, who shares my fantasies; Beverly, whose support transcends any distance; and my agent, Charlotte Sheedy, whose patient advice was invaluable.

Finally, I thank my friend Michael—for employing me, elevating me, bringing me songs—and for enduring

1.
What's All This Talk About "Assertiveness?"

There's no doubting it, the years just before "adulthood" are the strangest, most confusing, muddiest times anyone will endure. A German poet called those years "the May of life," but when I think back on my own youth—and I don't go back *that* far, I'm not yet thirty—it seems more like a cold January.

I could have used this book, ten years ago.

Everything in life has a question mark attached to it now, and it all seems uphill: What am I preparing for? Am I doing the right things to get ready? Can I be loved and still be me? Am I worth loving in the first place? What am I about? And when will things stop being such an enormous hassle?

No generation before has grown up in a world quite so fast-paced or open, and just getting by can make a person dizzy. We wonder if *the way we act* with people could make a difference—"they" say it does, but somehow we're always doing or saying things we don't want to, and we aren't sure why that happens. We know we can question traditions or ways of doing things which don't seem reasonable to us, but no one ever told us how to do that without making people mad. Somewhere in the confusion, we're expected to come up with an identity—a good idea of "Who I am; what I want to give to (and take from) my own future."

How does it all happen? I remember thinking as a teen-ager that if I could somehow make it through these years when everyone is telling me what's best for me, and what I'm good at, and what I should be working toward, things would ease up. By the time I would reach my twenties, everything would be ironed out—settled—and the world would be off my back.

It doesn't automatically work that way, and this is why. Our days are full of what we call "anxiety situations." These anxiety situations can be big events—getting suspended from school, ending a friendship, or a death in the family, for instance. More often, though, they are smaller happenings that make us feel uncomfortable, and we aren't quite sure how to act.

What happens then? Well, if we have not yet learned how to behave assertively and directly, we allow someone *else* to decide how we will behave.

Sometimes, we're not even *aware* that some situations make us anxious or uncertain about how we should act. I have listed five minor but common situations that call for assertive actions. Read them, and think about how you would react if these things happened to you.

When you're finished, we can begin—*slowly*—talking about what assertiveness is, when we need it, and how it can make things easier. With this short quiz, the idea is to try to be *aware* of the feelings, tensions, and types of relationships going on—how they affect each other, and how all of the dynamics ("vibes") would change if the parties involved behaved differently toward each other.

After you've read more about different kinds of relationships—and how to make yourself aware that in some instances, with certain people, different ways of behaving are called for—there will be more quizzes. Later, you can look back at your old test scores and see how far you have come, as you work your way through the book. If you are using this book in a class or workshop, discuss these situations and similar ones you've been in, how you reacted, and, if you came out of it feeling lousy for some reason, how you might have handled things differently.

WHAT WOULD YOU DO?

1. You've become a close friend with a girl named Jan. She understands your feelings better than almost anyone you've ever known; you disagree sometimes, but for some reason, when Jan criticizes you, it's easier to accept the criticism, or tell her you think she's wrong. All in all, you feel that Jan is good for you, and you're glad that she's your friend.

   Your parents don't see it that way. Jan's parents are divorced and Jan has much more freedom than you. In fact, you have argued with your folks because you're not as free to do things as she is. Her clothes, which aren't very nice anyway, are usually wrinkled. Yesterday your mother saw Jan in the park holding hands with a boy, and both were smoking cigarettes. That was the last straw—you were told never to see or talk on the phone with Jan again. You:

   a. Have a big fight with your parents and stomp off to your room crying, making sure they know how much they hurt you. Then, continue to sneak and see Jan when you can.

   b. Calmly explain to your parents how much her friendship means to you, and help them to understand how hard she tries, in spite of her messed-up home life. If they don't understand, go along with their wishes and stop seeing Jan.

   c. Talk to your parents as in (b), but continue to be Jan's friend if they don't understand.

   d. Accept from the start that parents do know what's best in the long run, and tell Jan you can't see her anymore.

2. There is a boy (or girl, if you are a boy) whom you like a lot, but don't know very well yet. You watch things he (or she) does, and more and more, you wish you could get closer. Every time you talk to this person, though, it's in a group of other friends, and you don't want to tell him/her how you feel, in front of an audience. For that matter, you're pretty nervous about doing it under any conditions. But it's driving you crazy, and you have to do *something* and get it over with. You:

   a. Call the person on the phone and ask him/her to come to your place to study for an evening, hoping a nice, "getting-to-know-you" talk will also happen.

   b. Call on the phone and tell the person you've noticed he or she likes to do some things you also enjoy. Talk about it a little, and suggest that you do them together sometime.

   c. Decide that if he or she wanted to spend time with you, you would have *been* asked by now, and let it go, rather than risk being turned down.

   d. Write a friendly letter, saying that you'd like to know the person better, and why.

3. You saved your spending money for a month, till you finally had enough to buy a certain shirt you really love. The first time you wear your new shirt, you notice a tear in the shoulder, and you take it back the next day. The store clerk, though, won't return your money because you did wear the shirt once, and says you should have examined it better before you bought it. You:

   a. Agree that you didn't look as carefully at the shirt as you should have, so you take it home and mend it as well as you can.

b. Insist—until you're screaming, if necessary—that the store should stand behind its products, a shirt should last more than one day, and you're not leaving the store without your money.

c. Calmly insist that a shirt for sale should be wearable, and since this one is not, you want your money back. When the clerk keeps refusing, tell her—a hundred times, if you have to, but always quietly and calmly —that you understand her position, but you want your money back.

d. Throw the torn shirt on the counter, pick up a good one, and walk out of the store.

4. You just got your driver's license, and your parents let you borrow their car to take some friends to the movies. No one can decide which movie to see. You spend half an hour driving around, wasting gas. All the time, you're thinking of a new, sort of corny movie you'd like to see, but nobody's suggested that one at all, and you don't think they'd like it. Still, you're sick of driving around and are getting fed up with the whole evening. You:

a. Pull the car over to the side of the road and announce that you're not driving another block until someone decides.

b. Suggest seeing the corny movie, offering to buy the popcorn if everyone will agree.

c. Suggest seeing the corny movie, then get all of the suggestions narrowed down to two "finalists," vote, and get to the movie before it's too late.

d. Drive to the theater where one of the suggested movies is playing and tell your friends that this is what they will see.

5. For your school's Christmas program, you recited a long poem you had written. You had never let anyone hear your poetry before, and you weren't sure how an audience of high school students would react. But you

worked hard to make it perfect, and had a friend play her flute in the background for added effect. After the program there were lots of quick compliments, and it was easy to rattle off a dozen quick "thank-yous." But when your English teacher took you aside and told you it was much better than she'd expected—good enough to be published somewhere, in fact—and that she'd like to look at more of your poetry, you felt awkward and embarrassed. You:

a. Reply that this poem went over OK, but you really don't think the rest of your stuff is ready to be seen yet.

b. Thank her for her confidence, and tell her you'd like her to look at your other poems if she could set aside the time to *really* read them carefully, and tell you how they could be improved.

c. Thank her, but point out that the flute in the background made your words sound better than they really are.

d. Thank her, but point out how hard you had to work to get the words just right, because no teacher ever had the time to teach you how.

Answers

1. This is one of the most delicate issues every adult has to iron out: How far will I go for what I believe in? Is it a question of guts, or loyalty, or what? It's a heartbreaking plight; your decision is to betray either your parents or a valuable friend. Some choice.

    On the other hand, it's not until we put our feelings to the test, in real life, that we know for sure what we're made of.

    At this point—living in your parents' home, allowing them to take care of your needs—your primary allegiance has to be to them, *but not all* of your allegiance. The most workable answer is (b), but the most important part of (b) is explaining the situation to your folks—why Jan is important to you, how she helps you, how you know she's a good person to be close to. If you can't convince them, you also owe it to Jan to have a long talk. It's all right to tell her how you've been pressured by your parents into making this painful decision, and that you do care for her more than any other friend you've had. But be honest, too, and make it clear that the decision to go along with your parents' feelings was made by *you*. Most parents wouldn't object if you associated with your friend at school.

Answering (c) would get you two things: You would continue seeing Jan, and your parents would *think* you're following their wishes. But how would *you* feel about what you were doing? One of the most painful things about moving into adulthood is being a person of *honor*. It's painful because it can mean doing things that hurt you—like losing Jan's friendship to keep your parents' trust. But it's not possible to be a person of honor *and* be a person who sneaks when authority turns its back. You've just got to be one or the other.

If you answered (a) or (d), you would rather take the easy way out than deal with the problems in your life. In the first answer, you're throwing a tantrum to make your parents feel guilty about how they treat you. In the second, though your folks might know best, you haven't even asked why. What can you tell Jan to comfort her as you abandon her, if you and your parents haven't even talked it out?

2. Answer (a) isn't a bad approach, but (b) is the best answer because you accomplish a lot more. Getting acquainted is awkward enough, without your family's traipsing through the room, listening to every word. Having a brief phone conversation, then doing something together that you both enjoy, will break the ice

more quickly and more naturally. Answer (c) is an obvious cop-out; there's a good chance the other person is thinking the same thing and figures *you're* not interested.

Writing a letter as in (d) is an acceptable way of expressing your thoughts much *later* in the relationship, as well as being terrific therapy. I often write letters to friends who live nearby, just to sort out thoughts I'm having. But writing without really knowing the person is another cop-out. You can't make friends unless you're willing to *talk* with people; let them know up front what you are like.

3. Answer (a) completely ignores your rights as a consumer. Though you may not always get your way when you deal with salespeople, remember one cardinal rule: It is *never* "your fault" when you buy something defective (unless the salesperson tells you about the defect—flaw—before you pay for it), so don't be scared into thinking *you* did something wrong when you bought the article. Assertiveness does not, however, mean getting yourself arrested, which could happen if you picked (d).

What you say in (b) is true, but screaming won't get your money back. The most workable answer is (c), in which you've utilized an important skill called the Echo Skill (see page 42). You're much more likely to convince the clerk that you are right, if you do two important things: One, keep your cool, and two, keep repeating your main point (in this case, "I want my money back") each time you speak. Repeat it over and over, until you sound like an echo that won't go away.

4. Both (a) and (d) are *aggressive,* not assertive. You've given your friends an ultimatum—"This is what you'll do, or else"—and that will only make everyone angry at you and ruin an already-tense evening. In (b) you are being *passive*—instead of directly suggesting your

movie, you feel as though your opinion isn't as important as theirs. So you buy the popcorn, as though their considering your choice is a big favor to you.

The best way to handle the situation is (c). Throw your suggestion in as though it was equal to all the others (which it is), take a vote, and agree that everyone will go along with the majority. This is *compromise*, a sort of give-and-take, bargaining process, and it saves a lot of time and tempers if it's used as soon as the need for it is recognized.

5. It may be true, as in (a), that you hadn't worked as hard on the poems at home as you did on this one, and you don't think they're good enough for people to read yet. But your teacher isn't interested in a book to curl up with at night—she's telling you that you are competent at writing poetry, maybe even good. By showing her your other work, you might learn how to bolster the weak points in your poetry. This isn't the time for false shyness—you might not get another chance for free, professional help from a genuinely concerned person. Take your teacher up on her offer, as in (b). After all, you don't *have* to use her suggestions.

If you chose (c), you need more confidence in yourself, so that you won't feel the urge to put yourself down a little bit when you receive compliments. Answer (d) is defensive and rude.

TYPES OF RELATIONSHIPS

A relationship refers to the way you "connect" with different people. Parents are a different kind of relationship than are best friends, for instance, though both are close to you. You can see from the above questions that there are different "kinds" of people you have to deal with:

Formal Relationships

A clerk in a store has a formal relationship with you; so does a waiter in a restaurant. The rules of these relationships are pretty much set down before you ever meet. If it is a smooth relationship, the other person performs a service (rings up something you bought, serves you food in a restaurant, washes your car, and so on) and you pay for it.

Problems happen in formal relationships when one person or the other fails to hold up his or her part of the understood bargain. Most of the time, the problem can be easily corrected (returning the torn shirt, for example) and both of you go your separate ways.

Sometimes, though, a person in a formal relationship (or any other kind of relationship) can *manipulate* you into thinking that you were wrong, or guilty in some way. We will talk about *manipulation* over and over again in this book, because it's what stops most people from becoming *assertive*.

Let's go back to question (3) of the quiz for a minute. If you believe the store clerk when she says you should have examined the shirt more carefully, she has *manipulated* you into thinking you did something *wrong*. Instead of the store's being at fault, *you* are—it's *your* fault, not the store's, that you now own a torn shirt.

Authority Relationships

Other types of people with whom you connect are those in a position of authority over you: Parents, teachers, and "your elders" are the most obvious examples.

In these connections, or relationships, the rules are very clear. The teacher's job is to present new information to you, and your role is to take in as much as you can. Even more clear are the rules that govern your relationship with your parents. Whole chapters will be devoted to family and authority. For now, we want to understand the *different ways we act* around certain people and how we feel about our dealings with certain ones. By the time you finish chapter one, you will have thought a lot about this and begun to figure out which ways of dealing with people, or *your own behavior,* you want to change.

For most people under twenty-one, hassles with parents center around freedom. Maybe you can accept the fact that you have to wash dishes, but you want to put it off for an hour, and Mom wants them done *right now.* You could come up with a hundred tiny examples.

The point is that you are ready to make *some* decisions now, and your parents might not be ready to *let* you. Acting assertively with your parents is very different from acting assertively with your friends, because you don't *depend* on your friends for things. Still, you can be *direct* with your parents, and that's the first—and biggest—step.

Being direct with parents is more than telling them what you feel or want. It must be done in a way that will make them *listen* to you. They listen a lot more easily if you're talking calmly, and giving good reasons for what you want, than if you're throwing a tantrum.

Manipulation happens a lot between parents and their sons and daughters. We try to make our parents feel guilty if they don't do (or don't let *us* do) what we want. On the other hand, they can make us feel guilty or bad if we make mistakes, or don't do something as well as other people's kids.

You should remember, though, that *no one can make* you feel guilty. You only feel guilty, or "not as good" somehow, *if you believe people who say you're not as good.* If you feel like that a lot of the time, then you already know that you need more self-confidence, and will want to pay special attention to chapters four and six.

Brothers, sisters, and friends connect with us on a more or less equal basis. Some brother/sister relationships, though, might be mixed with some authority; a lot of us had to listen to the "older kids" in the family.

In equal relationships, we are more free to help make up the rules. Also, if you and the other person can't agree on how you will act toward each other, you can (unless it's a brother or sister) end the relationship entirely, if that's what you choose to do.

Equal relationships, especially with friends, are good places in which to "practice" being assertive, because you have more *control* in these. There are some things that parents want us to do, that we *have* to go along with, no matter how much we (calmly) reason with them that it doesn't make sense to us. With friends, though, we can *choose* to go along or not to go along; we don't even have to have a good reason. In equal relationships, we are most free to use assertiveness Skills, which you will read about in chapter two, to solve problems with the other person.

WHAT WE SHOULD REMEMBER

The important thing to remember about types of relationships is that we do *behave differently* around different people. Some of us are confident and satisfied with the way we act around teachers, but don't get our point across very well when we debate things with brothers or sisters; they "walk all over us." Or vice versa.

In chapter eight, we'll learn how to "fatten our awareness." You've heard of fattening your belly, right? Well, our heads need food, too, and storing up facts isn't the total solution to feeding your head. Sometimes, we need a different kind of information to be able to make the decisions that will work best. We need to be able to use our *senses,* not just hard facts, to know what's happening and why people act the way they do. We'll learn how to be *aware,* and do some exercises that will make it even easier to zero in on what we want to change about ourselves and the way we act.

Keep in mind that *if you are satisfied* with the way you behave or respond in some situations, *there is no need to change.* Seeing the difference between authority, formal, and equal relationships is a first step. It should help you to sort out the ways you act when you're with certain people, and how you feel about what happens in those relationships. If you're pretty much satisfied with the way you feel and act with some people, *don't* change. Go on to other sections that will help you more.

EXERCISE

This exercise is to make sure you understand the different ways in which you relate to "types" of people in your everyday life. Learning how to be assertive with other people will be a lot easier if you're first aware of how you react to them.

Fill in this chart for one week. Include *every* contact you have with other people, no matter how brief or unim-

Date	Person	Type of Relation-ship	Situation	What Satis-fied Me about How I Acted	What I Didn't Like about My Behavior	My Over-all Feeling about the Contact—Good, Bad

portant it seems, and add as many extra pages as you need. At the end of the week, review your performance, and be very honest with yourself about what you would like to improve. Don't wait until the end of the week to go to the next section, but *do* keep your chart with you, recording your contacts with people as soon as they happen.

When you're looking over the chart a week from now, keep an eye open for *repeats:* Were you usually more satisfied after contacts with one type of relationship than with the others? With whom did "anxiety situations" come up? What happened in those instances, and how did your anxiety (feeling uncomfortable, unhappy, walked on) show itself to the other person?

WHAT AM I IN FOR?

Assertiveness, if you haven't caught on yet, is sort of the opposite of anxiety, or perhaps the absence of it. No one really *possesses* assertiveness. It's a skill, like typing or dribbling a basketball, which a person first *learns*, then *practices*, every day, in order to keep on being good at it.

When you can finally say, "I'm an assertive person!" these three things will also be true about you:

1. You can act and talk *directly* with all relationships in your life, without being afraid or making excuses for for what you do. If you are nervous (anxious) in a situation, the other person can't tell. And, when you are wrong or make a mistake, you take your own lumps without feeling as if you just got shafted.
2. When you want something, or want a certain thing to happen to you, or wish a specific thing were true about you, *you* take steps to see that it comes true. You don't wait for it to happen, or hope that someone will read your mind and take care of it.
3. Whether you get what you want, get only part of it, or

lose completely—when it's over, you always have the satisfaction of saying, "I did what I could. I *like* the way I acted. Even if I didn't end up with what I want, I sure tried and it's not my fault. Besides, I learned something. Above all, because of the way I handled things, *I LIKE ME.*"

EXERCISE

This exercise will help you to learn if the three characteristics of an assertive person are true about you, and which you need to work on.

Choose three contact situations from your relationship chart. (Of course, you'll have to wait until the chart is at least partially filled.) One situation should correspond with the first characteristic of an assertive person, so pick a contact in which you acted nervous or anxious, or felt stepped on, and showed it.

The second situation should be a recent time when you *wished* a certain thing were true about you, or would happen to you, instead of doing something about it.

For the third, pick any situation in which you didn't like the way you acted, or later wished you had done something differently.

After you have selected your test situations, do some hard thinking about each. Why were you nervous in the first case; with whom were you speaking? Does that person always make you anxious? Why? What were you envious about in the second situation, or what were you wishing for? Is there anything you can do about it, without hurting someone? If not, why waste energy worrying about it?

In the third case, what don't you like about the way you acted? Do you do it often? What could you have done differently, to like yourself and your behavior a little more?

Act out each of the three situations alone in your room, trying out different *alternative* behaviors, until you know exactly how you'll act if those things happen again. Write your three solutions down and talk them over with a good friend, somebody with whom you talk about important or personal things. You don't have to make a big issue of it; just say something like, "Listen, these three things happened to me recently. I'll tell you how I acted, then I'll tell you what I think would have been a *better* thing to do, and you tell me what you think about it."

You'll find that support from a friend, especially now when you are beginning to be assertive and control parts of your life that others used to control, will help a lot. Even if your friend doesn't agree with all of your solutions, just *talking* about being assertive, or in control of the way you act, will help you *feel* more confident about yourself. Assertiveness is a little contagious, too—besides giving an opinion on your solutions, your friend might end up doing some thinking about his or her own behavior!

YOU ARE WHAT YOU FEEL

This book begins where *you* are, in those tangled-up years that will define you as a person for some time to come. Together we will learn—as slowly and carefully as *you* wish—how to handle what is laid on you *now*, not what you can expect to encounter when you're forty. Our journey will be based on two very important facts:

How you see yourself is based on what you do. Think about that for a minute. Isn't it true that the more you stand up for yourself, and act the way you like other people to act toward you, the more you like and respect yourself? On the other hand, when you aren't happy with something you just did or said, don't you get a little depressed and down on yourself?

Behaviors—ways of acting—don't exist one at a time.

The things you do and say every day have a sort of buildup, or "cumulative," effect. If we were to draw a picture of your actions, and how your feelings toward your behaviors build up, it would look like this:

"HOW-TO-FEEL-BAD-FOREVER SPIRAL"

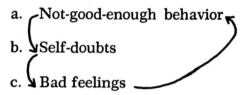

a. Not-good-enough behavior

b. Self-doubts

c. Bad feelings

We've all gone through this. We make a mistake, (a). We wonder if we can do anything right, (b). We feel so lousy about ourselves, (c), that the next time we're in a similar situation, we remember that we're not good enough to handle it, and so we don't, (a)—again.

A "spiral" is something that *continues* around a central point, like a coil. The central point is you, but your behavior does *not* have to act like a neurotic coil. When assertive people make a mistake, in fact, this chart doesn't apply to their behavior after they pass point (a). They don't go on to wonder if they're OK, or feel depressed, or feel afraid to be in that situation again.

An assertive person's "spiral" would look more like this:

"ASSERTIVE-BUILDUP SPIRAL"

a. Action—either mistake, or correct action

b. Ask self: What happened? What did I do?

c. Ask self: How do I feel about how *I* acted?

d. Plan for next, similar situations

You can see that in this chart, self-punishing phrases like "not good enough" and "self-doubt" are not used. Instead, what happens is a sort of question-and-answer session with yourself, in which you are constantly *aware* of how you act and respond to other people. Then, you decide if your behavior was appropriate (right for that situation), and how you feel about your behavior. If the way in which he or she acted wasn't appropriate, the assertive person looks at other possible solutions to the problem—not feeling guilty, or putting one's self down; just drumming up other ways of handling the situation.

This question-and-answer session with yourself is called "weighing" or "evaluating the alternatives" (choices), and it should happen each time you make a decision, no matter how unimportant it seems. Most choices, if you think about it, are between something *you* want to do, and what someone *else* thinks you should do. We all have to do many, many things we don't want to do, of course, but at least by evaluating the situation we can understand *why* some things are necessary, and that makes them a little less painful.

If you're not sure whether a certain way of responding would be "assertive" or not, remember the three things that we said would be true of an assertive person. Then, simply ask yourself: "Would I feel better *about myself* if I did (or said) that? Or would I feel better *about myself* if I chose another alternative instead?"

WHAT'S YOUR B.Q. (BUILDUP QUOTIENT)?

All of our behavior is cumulative, or has a buildup effect, influencing our *next* behaviors. How does yours build? Do you look at your behavior and feel guilty and inadequate, or do you use it to keep improving yourself?

Make two "spiral" charts of your own. Pick a problem in your life that makes you feel depressed or "not good enough," one in which you keep repeating your old, unsatisfying behavior that makes you feel badly about *yourself*. Here's an example:

My not-good-enough
   action: I got a C on my oral report.

Self-doubts: Maybe I did deserve a bad grade. Maybe I should have done it like Bill or Cindy. Maybe I should have worn a nicer outfit. Maybe I looked and sounded like an idiot up there.

Bad feelings: I am bad at giving oral reports, and I hate giving them. It's not fair to make me do it, and I'm afraid to do it again.

Now, take that same problem and find a solution, as in the following example. Figure out what sorts of behaviors you might use that would make you *feel good about yourself* in solving your problems, like this:

Action: I gave an oral report in class and received a C grade.

Ask self: What happened? Alternatives might be: (a) the content of my talk was incomplete; (b) I was too nervous to deliver the report well, and it showed; (c) teacher doesn't think I worked hard enough—did I? (d) Report was under or over the set time limit; (e) I was bored with the topic, and the class could tell.

Ask self: How do I feel about *my* behavior? If I thought the C grade was unfair, did I do or say anything to the teacher about it? Did I do it in a way that makes me satisfied with my behavior and make the teacher listen to and respect what I had to say, whether she ends up changing my grade or not?

Next time: Base this on the answers to the questions you just asked yourself.

BACK TO YOU, PERSON

We still haven't "zeroed in" on all of your nonassertive behaviors in our general examples. It's not hard to figure out why we *don't* act assertively sometimes. It's simply the easiest way out. By not expressing ourselves, we avoid responsibility for the things we say and do.

Still, you are getting ready to take on some of that responsibility, and don't want to depend on your family and others to guide your behaviors. Before you begin to take things into your own hands, though, you need to have an idea of where you might want to go. And before you can even begin to think about that, you have to know who you are.

The quiz below will help you to do that. There are no "right" or "wrong" answers. The idea is to take some time, a whole day if you need it, and answer these questions. Get into your own head, spend the time alone, and figure out where you're really coming from.

As you answer the questions, you'll become even more aware of ways in which you want to improve, people you have trouble asserting yourself with, and how often you become anxious or upset. You'll also learn, of course, which behaviors and situations you feel perfectly confident and *satisfied with,* and don't need to change, because they make you feel good about yourself. Keep this distinction in mind as you go through the questions—which behaviors make you *feel badly about yourself* and which make you *like* yourself.

Take your time, and above all, *be honest with yourself*.

GETTING TO KNOW ME

1. Do you offer your opinions in groups of older people, and can you disagree in such groups? What happens if you try, and how do you react? What would you like to change about how you act when you're with older people?
2. Have you ever received awards for anything? How did you feel? How did you act? How do you feel and act if you don't win an award you think you deserve?
3. Would you ever go out with a group of friends if you were the only one without a "date"? If yes, how do you feel when you do it? If not, what do you feel that makes you say no?
4. Do you feel guilty asking someone to return something he or she has borrowed from you? How do you react if it is damaged?
5. How do you react when you receive a compliment? Does it embarrass you?
6. Have you ever told a member of the opposite sex that you "like" him or her? Is it difficult for you to be the one in a relationship to do or say something first?
7. How do you generally feel about people of your own sex? Do you feel supportive, or in competition with them? How would you rather feel?
8. Do you ever lie about how you feel toward someone to avoid hurting his or her feelings? When you do, do you think that's the best way to handle things at the time, or are you really wishing you had the nerve to do something different?
9. Do you feel you're special in any way? Think about it—how?

10. How do you feel about very old people? How do you act around them?

11. How do you feel about your body? What about it embarrasses you, or don't you like?

12. Have you ever asked someone for a hug? If not, have you ever wanted to?

13. Who can make you feel fear? How do they do it?

14. Think about your parents' personalities. If they were your age, would you choose them as friends? Why, or why not?

15. Does it scare you to wonder what you'll be doing five years from now? What are some of the possibilities you can imagine now?

16. Do you touch people of both sexes easily? Would you like to be more (or less) affectionate than you are?

17. Do you have platonic friendships (friendships with persons of the opposite sex which aren't romantic relationships)? What are (or would be) some of the benefits of friendships like that?

18. What do people do that hurts you?

19. What traits in others do you admire or wish you had? What could you do to develop those traits for yourself? Will you?

20. What about you do you feel is "masculine" or "feminine"? Have you ever been judged, for any reason, on that basis? Does it make sense?

21. Do you feel that you *should* get married someday?

22. What is there about your parents' relationship that you would do differently if you were married?

23. What is love to you? What do you expect from it? What different "kinds" of love—whatever that means to you—do you give and get at this point in your life?

24. Do you ever change your mind to get people's approval? How do you feel about yourself when you do?

25. Do you ever try to make your parents feel guilty? In what situations?

26. Do you ever read other people's mail, diaries, or other private materials? If so, what do you get out of doing it? How does it make you feel toward yourself?

27. Does it bother you when people watch you work? In what way? Do you express your feelings when they do it?

28. Is it hard for you to give people compliments? Which people? Why do you think that happens?

29. What do you think you will gain by becoming more assertive? What do you think has stopped you from being direct with people in the past?

30. How important is religion in your life?

31. What do you feel most ashamed of in your past?

32. Have you ever experienced sex? Do you practice masturbation? How do you feel about both at this point in your life?

33. How do you feel about interracial dating or marriages?

34. How important is money to you?

35. What do you like most about your body?

36. Do you drink, smoke marijuana, or use other drugs? How do you feel about all three, or about people who use them?

37. Do you enjoy manipulating or directing people to act in a way you want them to, rather than the way they already do?

38. Have you ever been tempted to kill yourself? Someone else? Who, and why? Does it bother you to think about it now? In what way?

39. Would you participate in a public demonstration? If so, what issues do you feel strongly enough about to do it?

40. What is your most serious problem at the present time? Can you think of possible, alternative ways to solve it? Will you have to change your own behavior to pull it off?

41. What do you daydream about the most?

42. How do you feel about crying in front of other people?

43. Do you like your name? If not, why? What name would you like to have instead of your own?

FOLLOWING THROUGH

Now that you've taken the time to explore yourself, here is an even more difficult—but most important, so don't skip it—assignment.

Take a tablet (not just a single sheet of paper, you'll need at least several pages) and at the top of the first page, write the title: "Everything That Matters about (your name)." Then, based on what you learned about yourself in the above quiz, write a profile of *you*. Write and write and write till it's all on paper, out of your system—what you like, who hurts you, everything that matters, good and bad.

This may be difficult, because most people have never been forced to confront themselves so completely. You may find yourself admitting things for the first time, things that would seem silly or embarrassing if anyone else were to find them out. If it's any consolation, I went through every exercise in this book as I was writing it, and some of them weren't so easy—including this one. But each one meant one more accomplishment and made me like myself a little more.

Keep writing until you think you've said everything about you that matters. Then, share it—with ONE person. Pick a friend or family member you feel very close to, and read your profile out loud. If you are using this book as a text in a class or assertiveness workshop, split into dyads (groups of two people) and read to each other. Do *not* read your profile to a whole group of people. The idea is to *declare yourself*, say, "This is me, and it's just fine," to *one* person who cares that you are you, and cares that you like being you. Then, take a breather and congratulate yourself. You've just let someone "in," and that's something that many people never accomplish in their entire lifetime.

2.

Everyone Has Rights

You will be reminded of your Rights and Skills over and over, throughout this book. For now, we'll just become acquainted with what they are. In other chapters, you will learn more about how to apply them in different situations, with different types of relationships—friends, parents, strangers. You will remember your *Rights,* and you'll learn to recognize immediately if someone is trying to step on them. Your *Skills* will help you to assert those Rights.

To understand how Rights and Skills relate to each other, think of the phrase "law enforcement." Laws are rules by which we live; they were made up by elected legislators. The enforcement of those laws—asserting them, handling the situation when a law is broken—is in the hands of enforcers, usually police officers.

Rights and Skills work in the same way. Rights are *theories,* rules by which *you* live. The Skills we will learn are *behaviors,* ways in which *you will act* in order to uphold your Rights.

Why do we need to learn our Rights and Skills? Simply, because *not* learning how to stand up and protect our

Rights can keep us from doing and getting what we want, for the rest of our lives. It is with this section that you will truly start to *change your behavior*, getting rid of those ways of doing things that *you* have decided are bad for you—things that hold you back or keep you down.

RIGHTS

We will go through your Rights as a person, one by one. As you read the explanation of each Right, jot down one situation in your life when you felt that that particular Right was stepped on by someone else. That "someone else" can be from any type of relationship: formal, as a store clerk; authority, as a teacher or parent; or equal. It does, though, have to be a real person with whom you have come in contact. You will use this list for an exercise that follows the Rights and Skills.

Right No. 1: You have the right to be your own judge—to do what you decide to do, and then be responsible for the consequences.

In order to assert this Right, *you* have to be the one to *take* the responsibility for your actions away from people who are used to your depending on them.

Some people think that you should be controlled. In fact, since you have not yet reached the "age of majority" and are living in a home owned by someone else—your parents—your providers do also have rights regarding your behavior. This is dealt with more thoroughly in chapter three. For now, the main point is that the less you *depend* on people, the less they will be able—or have a right—to control you.

Your friends and other equal relationships might not like the idea of your taking responsibility for your own behavior. Most of the time, the reason for this is that they haven't yet started to be responsible for themselves.

They're probably afraid that if you control *yourself*, rather than depending on how other people think you should act, you will also want to start controlling *them.*

Make it clear to friends who feel threatened by your new confidence and assertiveness that this will not happen. Let them know that you are only figuring out the rules and behaviors by which *you* want to live, and that their own behavior is their own business—and their own responsbility.

TIP: Try to remember not to think so much in terms of whether the things you do are "right" or "wrong." Switch as often as you can (every time you think about it) to the principle of "this works for me, that doesn't." You will find yourself sort of making up your own "rules" as you go along, deciding that one behavior or answer works best in one situation with a particular relationship, and others work best in other situations. GOOD FOR YOU—you're *weighing the alternatives* when you do that!

REMINDER: Write down a situation in which someone else tried to decide what was best for you, when you think something else would have worked better. Keep your note handy.

Right No. 2: You have the right not to give excuses for the things you do.

A friend might say to you, "Now, why did you go and do a stupid thing like that?" How else can you respond, but to try to give a clumsy explanation for what you did, which is supposed to represent what you are?

There are lots of other ways to handle a judgmental question like that. You can agree that you made a mistake, or you can simply answer, "Well, I did, and now I'll accept the consequences." Or, "It seemed right" is a good enough—in fact, about the best—reason for doing anything.

Never, though, should you agree that what you did

was "stupid," just because someone said so, nor do you need to *justify* your actions by explaining the "whys." The judge is *you,* remember? (Unless, of course, what you did was illegal and you're in Juvenile Court, in front of a real judge!)

TIP: The Skills that follow will give you many methods of dealing with people who always want to know *why* you did something. If this happens to you often, keep Right No. 2 in mind while you read the Skills, and try to connect them in your head as you read.

REMINDER: Write down the names of one or two people who always want to know "why you did that," keeping in mind which type of relationship he or she is to you.

Right No. 3: You have the right to change your mind.

When you decide to do something, you do so because it seems the best way to handle *that* particular situation. That doesn't mean that you will choose the same action in another situation, whether the same people are involved or not.

Changing your mind does *not* mean you are immature or irresponsible. It means that you are open to accepting new ideas and new ways of doing things.

For example, I changed my major field of study in college five times before I finally graduated. Naturally, this wasn't smiled upon by anyone, not even by me. There was, however, simply no way to know if those other things weren't right for me, unless I tried them out. Then, when I learned that they would never work for me, I went on to try other things that caught my interest. The result? Many of my old school chums feel "stuck" in professions that literally bore them to tears; since I eliminated those alternatives that wouldn't work for me before I got stuck, I am in a profession that makes me happy. It wasn't easy, but I finally got there.

This does not mean that it's fine to change your mind at the last minute if people are counting on you, and we will deal with dependability more in the chapter on friendship. Again, you have to *weigh the alternatives.* If you have made a solid commitment to do something, and backing out would mean leaving someone stranded in one sense or another, it might be best to go ahead and accept the unfavorable consequences of your decision.

REMINDER: Write down several instances when you changed your mind and were criticized or put down for doing it, and the results.

Right No. 4: You have the right to say, "I don't know," or "I don't understand."

The best way to explain this Right would probably be to merely repeat it, over and over again. It's OK not to know the answer to a question, even if the question is "What will be the consequences if I do this?" Sometimes you *don't know* what the results of your actions will be, and all you can do is what "feels" best for you at the time. Naturally, you will make the wrong choice sometimes. But you will also accept the responsibility for making that mistake, and be able to make a better decision next time.

We learn by experience. At the same time, none of us is expected to be a mind reader. Whether you are dealing with a teacher who is giving instructions or a friend who is trying to explain some very important feelings, it's perfectly all right to stop them and say, "Wait a minute. I don't understand something."

REMINDER: Write down a time when you remember not knowing something and were afraid or embarrassed to say so. Also, write about an incident when you didn't understand something and were too embarrassed to let anyone know.

Right No. 5: You have the right to say, "I don't care."

For the rest of your life, you will know people who think *they* know what would make you a better person. Someone will always be more than happy to tell you that you should study harder, you should lose weight, you should wear a certain look in your clothes, and on and on.

You are your own judge. As such, only *you* can decide which things about you or your behavior need correcting. If others judge that something about you is a flaw, and you don't see anything wrong with it or are satisfied with it, you are entitled to tell them that *you do not care.*

REMINDER: Write down something about you or your behavior that you feel has been unnecessarily criticized— something that you felt no need or desire to change.

Hang on to your examples of situations in which your above Rights were stepped on, for the exercises that follow the Skills.

SKILLS

Remember, Rights are rules by which you live; Skills are behaviors or ways in which you act in order to assert and uphold your Rights. You will eventually reach the point where, in a difficult or anxious situation, a tiny light will go on in your head and you will say to yourself, "Just a minute, I have a *Right* to . . ." And just as automatically, you will remember and be able to use the *Skill* you choose, to bring the situation to a satisfactory conclusion.

Once you have mastered these Skills, the benefits will be obvious. The most important benefit will be your ability to tell the difference, without much trouble, between the *truths* in what people say about your behavior and *judgments* about it. You will know if someone is trying to *manipulate* you and make you feel guilty if you don't operate by *their* rules and standards. In other words, you'll know whether to thank people for their honest criticism, or whether they're trying to hand you a load of bull about yourself that just isn't true. Here are the Skills to help you assert your Rights:

Skill No. 1: The Echo.
The Echo Skill is used when other people seem to be ignoring what you are really saying, and trying to manipulate you. To use the Echo, you simply keep repeating your main point, a hundred times if you have to, until you sound like a persistent echo that won't go away.
EXAMPLE: Your friend Shirley wants you to go to a party Saturday night. You promised your mother that you would help her paint the bathroom, and since you've put it off for weeks, you intend to stay home and keep your promise.

Shirley: You really should go to the party with me.
You: Thanks for asking, but I'm staying home.
Shirley: I don't know who I'll go with now.
You: Well, I didn't promise you I'd go with you, but I did promise Mom I would help her out, so I'm staying home.
Shirley: You know, you don't go out enough. You act like you're sixty years old.
You: I know you want me to go, but I'm staying home.
Shirley: You'll be sorry; you'll miss a lot of fun.
You: Thanks again for asking and have a good time, but I'm going to stay home.

Notice two things about this example. First, you use the phrase "I'm staying home" each time you speak, like an echo. Second, you do *not* get angry, or loud, or defensive when Shirley insults you.
Reacting emotionally—yelling, or getting upset— might have been just the response that Shirley was look-

ing for, and it would have made you sound weak and vulnerable. Most important, if Shirley would have been able to bring out an *emotional* response in you, chances are you would have given in, and ended up *not* doing *what would work best for you* that night.

Sometimes, in dealing with authority relationships, the Echo Skill won't get you what you want. However, in those situations, if your "echo message" is "Listen to what I have to say," over and over—calmly and quietly, that in itself might be an accomplishment! Being listened to might be the only goal in your reach, if a parent is angry at you. But, being listened to also has a *cumulative* effect and will get you closer to scoring with that person, and with yourself), and getting what you really want, the more it happens.

Skills Nos. 2 and 3: Dropping and Picking Up Clues.

Dropping Clues and Picking Up Clues are conversational Skills, and are used together. Most of us need conversational ability in awkward moments with the opposite sex, so we'll refer to it often in chapter eight. Basically, these Skills give you the ability to talk about yourself, and help others feel comfortable in talking about themselves.

How often have you sat with someone you didn't know very well, unable to keep a good conversation going? Assertiveness, remember, isn't just *getting* what you want. First, you have to *communicate* your wishes effectively. If you can't read other people's minds (remember Right No. 4; *you* don't always know things), you can't expect them to be able to read yours!

Dropping and Picking Up Clues means just that. You listen for tidbits of information from the other person, or offer your own, which could lead to two-way talking. You ask if they've ever done or seen something related to what they just said, how they felt about it, and relate that to similar experiences of your own.

Here is an example, with the "clues" underlined:

You: I didn't think so many people could be squeezed into this tiny room; *I'm used to a lot more space.*

Other: Me, too, but *with a big family like mine,* you get used to having a lot of people around.

You: Oh, you come from a big family?

Other: Well, there are seven of us, not counting my married brother *and his family.*

You: My sister is married, too, with two kids. How did it make *you feel* to become an uncle (aunt)?

From that point, this conversation could go in a hundred different directions—how it changes Christmas to have tiny children around again, what you've learned about mixing marriage and a career from watching older brothers and sisters, and so on.

The key is to *listen* for the other person's clues, then *relate* them to your own life and drop clues of your own. Being a good conversationalist is a Skill that few people have mastered. Fortunately, its one that can be practiced all the time!

Skill No. 4: Clouding.

Clouding is a Skill that comes in handy in response to judgmental criticism. Essentially, what happens is that you answer *only the truth* in the other person's statement and "cloud over" the rest.

Often when others criticize you, they don't stop at the truth of the matter. They try to make you think that what you do, or say, or want, is "wrong" by their standards. Since you live by your own standards of what works best for you, though, there's no need even to respond to their attempts to *manipulate* you (make you feel guilty or "stupid" for what you do, so that you will change your ways).

Here is an example of Clouding:

Other: Come on, just go skiing with me once, you'll see how easy it is.
You: I know it must not be the hardest thing in the world, since so many people do it. No, thanks.
Other: Come on, it doesn't cost that much. I'll even pay your way this time and lend you my skis, OK?
You: I have enough money, but I'd rather spend it on something I'd enjoy doing. Thanks, but no.
Other: People will think you're a big baby if you never ski. I think you're scared, too.
You: I can see how people might think that. Thanks anyway.

Notice, in the example above, that you did *not*: (1) deny the truth in the other person's statements; (2) defend yourself against judgments that you might be a "baby"; or (3) attack the other person. You simply agreed with the truth in each statement, and let it go at that.

This Skill is called "Clouding" because, in your mind, you "cloud out" or *ignore* the *judgments* people make, and respond only to what they've said that is true.

Clouding is an especially valuable Skill in that it teaches you to *really listen* to what people are *actually saying* to you, instead of what you *think* they mean by their remarks. Respond only to the *truth* in what they say, not what you imagine they might be implying, and it will be almost impossible for judgmental criticism to end up as an argument. In fact, Clouding usually stops it cold, after a few sentences.

Other Skills can be worked into the practice of Clouding. For instance, a friend criticizes your hairstyle. The truth is, you don't like it either and have considered getting a frizzy permanent. As you are responding only to the *truth* in your friend's criticism—the fact that your hair is not suited to you—and clouding out other judgments about how you look, ask a few questions. Do it calmly, without apologizing for yourself or criticizing your friend. Merely prompt him or her for some answers: Do frizzy permanents work on "fine" hair like yours? Wonder how much it might cost?

In *all* instances, *never* behave as though criticism is something about which to become depressed or upset, because it is not. Respond to the truths in people's statements, calmly telling them you agree or disagree. Ask for their opinions *if you want them*. But never, *ever* apologize or act as though what you are is "wrong"—it is not. You are only *different* from other people, and some of them will always want to change you. YOU ARE THE JUDGE of which of your characteristics will, or will not, be changed.

EXERCISE NO. 1

List ten things about you that have been criticized or that other people have said you "should" change. Make number one a very minor criticism, working up in importance to number ten, which is a criticism that really hurts you.

Then, pick out the *actual truths* in each of these criticisms. Imagine the conversations that actually happen with those persons as you do this. Spend an hour alone, making up "Clouding" conversations for each. (It's not necessary to write them down.) Pretend you are talking to the person who aims each criticism at you most often, and don't be afraid to talk out loud to yourself as you do it.

The next time you hear these judgmental criticisms, *use* these conversations you made up and practiced. Breathe deeply and talk slowly and calmly as you respond to only the *truth*, reminding yourself *not to deny the truth*, and *not to apologize*. You will see that once you sort out the truths about these criticisms ahead of time, in practice, *you will* remember them when you are criticized the same way again, and your calm, "Clouding" response will come out more easily then you expected.

EXERCISE NO. 2

As you were learning your Rights, you kept a list of situations in which someone tried to infringe, or "step on," those Rights.

Take that list now, and next to each situation, write down a Skill (or combination of Skills) that could help you out in each instance.

As you did in the above exercise, practice alone, using different Skills to assert different Rights. Play around with them, "mixing and matching" various Skills and Rights until you come up with the combinations that will work best for you.

Try out your new Skills the next time you feel that your Rights are being stepped on. The more often you practice them—alone or in "real life"—the more naturally and smoothly the words will fall into place. It will be shaky the first few times; just keep at it.

Another, more interesting version of this exercise is to rehearse with a friend. Show your friend the list of situations in which your Rights were stepped on or abused, and you hang on to your list of Skills. Stage a make-believe conversation for each situation, trying out different Skills in each instance, till you come upon a solution to the problem that will satisfy you. Your friend might want to come up with a list of abused-Right situations of his or her own, so that the two of you can switch roles—you play the abuser then, while your friend tries out the Skills to try to solve his or her own problems.

Remember, assertiveness is a skill that must first be learned, then practiced every day. It *will* become automatic, and dealing with people—in all types of relationships—will become as natural and comfortable for you as getting dressed in the morning.

3.

Home,
Sweet Hassle

You think it makes sense, wanting to do your homework *after* the nine o'clock movie instead of before. After all, it's easier to concentrate when everyone else is asleep— not to mention the fact that you just don't feel like doing it now. But, you have no choice. Mom says, "Do it."

It's a bummer, wanting to make your own decisions, but living under your parents' thumb at the same time. One psychiatrist defined those years in which a person prepares to leave home as the period of time ". . . just before parents become people." From your point of view, he's right.

There are certain tasks you must perform, and you would like the freedom, at least, to decide when you'll get those things done. But there's more to it than a desire to set your own agenda. You want time to develop a position. You need some control over your existence, and you resent having to account for every move you make. A few years from now, all of your choices and feelings and relationships will have a shape, and that shape will represent your "philosophy of life." Today, unhappily, your world is molded by rules that were made up by other people.

This is a time of transition or big change in your life, and nowhere is the conflict felt more strongly than at home. Those changes in yourself—and in your parents, too—are a lot easier to take if you understand why they are necessary.

As a child, you had an unspoken agreement with your parents. The bargain was that, in exchange for their food, home, protection, guidance, and services such as clothes that were cleaned regularly, you would live by their rules. In short, you were *dependent* on them to take care of the things you needed.

Now that you are older and can manage more without their help, you are beginning to reject some of the rules, and you would like a little less of their guidance and protection, because it adds up to a lot of authority. You woud like to be more *independent*.

Something else is happening, though, which many of use don't realize because our parents never tell us. As you claim more responsibility for the things you do—independence—your parents have to *give up* some responsibility for your actions. Being responsible for you (taking care of you) is something your folks have done for many years, and they've got pretty used to it. Turning your life over to *you* might not be so easy for them. In other words, you're not the only one who is going through a time of difficult changes. It may mean acting very differently around your family than you used to act, but unless you show your parents that you understand that it's not always easy for them, either, they might not extend that understanding to you when *you* need it.

What does this mean in terms of getting what you want at home?

First, you may never "get what you want" from your parents, or from any other relationships you develop in your life. You are one person, responsible only for *your* behavior, and you cannot change—or be responsible for—

the behavior of others. And *your parents cannot possibly be anything but what they are.*

If you have not yet told your family that you are reading this book, now is the time to let them know. Explain that you are *not* trying to change the way your family does things, or cause any headaches. Your goal is to become a more effective and responsible person, who is able to cope with difficult situations and function in any group of people. Help your parents to understand that this project will *strengthen,* not weaken, all of your relationships, including those within the family. The following "Family Powwow" plan is a good way to introduce your entire family to these new ideas and goals.

EXERCISE

Talk first with each member of your family about having a Powwow. Tell them you'd like to let them in on a project that's very important to you, and set up a time and place when they can all be there. Sunday evening, when many families just relax, might be a good time to suggest.

Your family might be more receptive to the idea of your wanting to become an assertive person if you take the following approach:

1. Open with a statement that *invites* them to be a part of your new awareness, such as, "I'm doing some reading and thinking on this, and I'd like all of you to help me out with something."

2. Ask each member of your family to come up with *one* thing about the way you *behave*—not the way you look, or think, but the way you behave—that they do not like.

   VERY IMPORTANT: Make it clear to your family that you are not asking to be insulted, and that you're *not* necessarily planning to change your behavior to make them happy. Tell them, in fact, that you've been doing some serious thinking about how you handle yourself in different situations, and you *already* have a good idea of where your weaker points are, and what *you* would be happy changing in regard to your behavior.

The idea is, first, to open discussion between you and the rest of the family, and give everyone a chance to say what bugs them about the way the others behave. Families rarely bring up such complaints unless they are in the middle of an argument; the Family Powwow plan will bring those feelings out into the open in a much calmer, supportive atmosphere. The idea, you see, is to *help* each other, not to put each other down.

3. When they have finished airing their complaints about your behavior, you list *one* way each person acts that makes you unhappy.

4. Agree that no one will respond to the complaints against them just yet. Instead, each person will give some thought to why they behave in that way, and whether or not that way of acting makes *them* unhappy, too—that is, whether *they* (or you) feel like changing.

5. At the next Powwow, each person should talk about that behavior, and whether he or she wants to change— or if they like themselves the way they are.

6. Suggest that you go through this process every two weeks. Once every two weeks, your family would devote an hour or two to talking over your feelings about each other's behavior, and how you treat one another.

7. Remember that these talks don't have to center around complaints about each other. If you notice that a brother or sister has gone out of his or her way to be patient with you, or give you compliments, bring it up during the discussion. Congratulate each other on obvious attempts to treat each other as people, and let your family know that you appreciate their efforts to be kinder and more respectful to you.

8. It might be helpful to take this book to that first Pow-

wow session and pass it around. You could even start by reading this section aloud to your family, and asking for their reactions.

PARENTS ARE PEOPLE

Your assertiveness may not change your folks' behavior toward you. It will, however, show them that you are ready to be a little less dependent on them. They will see that you are *ready to move on from adolescence,* because you are beginning to *see them as people*—people with problems they don't always know how to solve, people who enjoy a good laugh, people who, like you, get hurt. This brings us to a second point: How can you understand your parents and see them as people if they don't always let you "in"?

Parents are proud. In order to make you believe that they have authority over you—which, incidentally, they do, as long as you accept goods and services (dependence) from them—they might hide their feelings from you. Still, in order to gain more freedom, you have to be responsible *without* hurting their feelings, or being sarcastic when you don't get your way, or trying to make them feel guilty. Understanding what it is to be a parent is simply the first step in *communicating effectively* with them. At least, if they see that you understand their side of things, they'll listen to what you have to say.

EXERCISE

This exercise will help you to see your parents as people, with feelings and identities separate from you.

1. Pretend that you are your father, and write an essay. The title of the essay will be "The Hard Times I Had, Raising _____ (your name) _____."

2. Write another essay with the same title, pretending that you are your mother.

As you write, remember that "hard times" doesn't *only* mean the difficult things your folks *did*. It also means the things they did *not* get to do—vacations alone or together, things they couldn't buy, having to be home early because of the kids, or not being able to just be alone in their own home for an evening.

Read the essays when you've finished writing. Do you feel as though you understand a little more about having children and living with them every day? Did this exercise trigger any second thoughts about being a parent yourself someday, or make you realize something you hadn't thought of before?

EXERCISE

Set up three chairs in your room. Sit in one of them, with the other two facing you. Pretend that your parents are in the other chairs, and begin "telling" them secrets. Talk mostly about thoughts and feelings you have had toward them, but would never tell them in person. Let it be a very calm, friendly, "adult" conversation. When you feel as though one of your parents would respond to something you've said, or have secret feelings of their own about you (good and bad), switch chairs and say those unspoken thoughts as your parents might say them, if they were really sitting there. Carry on this "conversation" for at least twenty minutes, even if you run out of things to say, and try to distinguish between those secret feelings about your parents that still seem important, now that you have them off your chest, and those that don't seem so important anymore.

Think about those feelings that still seem important after you said them out loud. How did your "parents" react to them in your practice talk? Would they respond the same way in real life? Would it improve your relationship with your parents to talk with them about these things? If so, pay special attention to the section on getting your parents to listen to you, and plan to talk those feelings over with them.

WHAT PRICE FREEDOM?

The nicest thing about having parents is that you are provided for and taken care of, and someone else does the worrying. There are advantages to being on your own, too. Unfortunately, you must accept *responsibility* before you can enjoy the biggest advantage: freedom.

How can a younger person begin to take on some responsibility? How can you begin to convince your parents that at least some of the things you say or think are worth listening to? When you say, "I'm ready to go on and do this," or, "I really *can* handle this myself," what can you do to convince them that what you're saying might be true?

The answer: *Get a job.*

You've heard that money speaks in all languages. If you are managing some money, providing for a few of your own needs, the message that people hear is that you are responsible. You know more than you used to know, you've experienced payment for services rendered, and you have become less dependent.

When you depend on your folks financially, it not only gives them a way of controlling you, it gives them—and this is hard to swallow—the *right* to control you. The rule goes like this: If parents pay for and take care of all that you need and want, they call the shots. When you want the freedom to call some of your own shots, you must also accept some of the responsibility for attending to your own needs. The most effective and impressive way to attend to your needs is to *pay for them yourself.*

Most parents would rather see their children able to handle their personal affairs, without getting hurt by the outside world. If you work part time, even if you earn only enough to cover your "spending money" expenses, your parents see that you *can* handle some things yourself. They worry a little less and loosen up a little bit. They respect you a little more, for wanting to make your own way. And, unless your parents have more dough than they can count, they'll like you a little more as a person, because paying for even a few of your own needs will be a favor to them.

EXERCISE: DECLARATION OF (FINANCIAL) INDEPENDENCE

In this exercise, you will work out a plan for providing for some of your own financial needs. There are many points to consider in this important project, and every person's family situation is different. So, you will have to do some serious thinking about what might work out best for you. As you go through each step, be sure to *weigh the alternatives* and think about the results of each action you take.

1. List all of the reasons why earning some money of your own would be a good thing for *you* to do. On what will you spend your money? Will you be saving it for something in particular or using it to finance a hobby or activity you enjoy often? How hard (and how many hours) will you have to work to earn enough for that purpose? In what ways will your family benefit from your part-time job?

2. List the obstacles or hardships caused by your working. Will it cut into your studies or free time too much? Are you too young or unskilled to earn the money you need? Will your family oppose the idea? In what ways? Could there be problems getting to and from the job?

3. If the problems listed in (2) seem too big to handle, revise your goals. Think of other ways to earn money, read magazines for summer job ideas, talk to friends. Think of jobs for which you might be qualified, how

available those jobs are in your city, and how much you would earn in them. Find out whether a working permit is required, and if you are eligible.

4. Prepare yourself by writing down all of the advantages and disadvantages, and present your plan to your parents. If you are nervous about doing this, rehearse alone first. Ask your folks to set aside enough time to have a nice talk about it, with no brothers or sisters around— just the three of you. Begin with the points you listed in (1), emphasizing the ways in which your part-time job would help them out. Talk calmly and firmly, so they will know you are serious about this.

5. Don't expect your parents to be overjoyed with your plan if you have never worked before. Have an answer ready—one that will make sense to *them*—for every objection you imagine they might raise. When they do object, reason with them calmly, and be ready to *compromise* or partly give in to their wishes. Make it clear, though, that you really do intend to earn some money somehow and that your plan is important to you. Let them understand that you wanted this talk to enlist their support and to ask for advice. Do your best to sound as though you are *all on the same side.*

6. If your parents absolutely put their foot down and refuse to let you work, drop it. At least they listened to you. Approach them again in six months, and have another talk. Next time, have even more reasons why you are responsible enough to hold a part-time job.

If you are a little older and have worked before, you have already tasted a degree of independence. You may be approaching graduation in the next year or two, and are having a "freedom fight" of a different nature than that of younger brothers or sisters. In your effort to gain more control over your life as you prepare to leave home, you should consider the following points:

Your parents now, more than at any other time, feel threatened and a little afraid about your "leaving the nest." This is because you can get into much more serious trouble than when you were in your early teen years. Yet, this is the time when you are laying the foundation for a permanent adult relationship with your parents, so getting along with them is especially crucial now. The word to remember is *compromise*.

As you read earlier, your financial dependence is a means of parental control. As you cease to depend on your parents, be open and honest about which emotional "strings" are attached to financial support. In other words, guide your relationship with your folks so that they don't threaten to withdraw necessary financial support every time you try to assert yourself. If everyone is honest, and aware of the *conditions* on which money is given, you can decide in each instance if the emotional price—lack of freedom—is too high for you to pay in exchange for their money.

GETTING PARENTS TO LISTEN

We all feel nervous about talking to our parents about certain things, especially if the subject is one that has caused them to be angry, or punish us, in the past. You can't stop anyone from being angry with you if they choose to do so, but you *can* behave in such a way that the chances of that happening are *less*.

When you want to discuss something with your parents and they don't want to listen, don't give up. Keep trying to get them to talk with you. Remember, you are *building a relationship* with them as people. The more often and maturely you can talk things over with them, the easier it will be to move from your present dependency when the time comes. Keep the following tips in mind:

● There will be times, after you have begun a talk, when your parents will prove your opinion to be wrong. You don't want these incidents thrown in your face the next time you try to express your feelings. To keep that from happening, do *not* belligerently lay your opinion on your folks as if your word were the gospel truth and you are daring them to challenge it. Simply *present* your side of the issue, calmly and firmly.

● If your parents are sitting, sit also. Sit up straight, but be comfortable, with both feet on the floor, so you will appear to be confident about your views. If they are standing, you stand—the idea is to keep your face at approximately the same height as theirs, so that no one "talks down" to anyone else.

● If you feel tensions arising during the talk, touch your mother's or father's arm or hand as you speak.

● Begin the talk with a sentence such as "I would appreciate it if you would *listen* to what I'm saying, because it's pretty important to me."

● Review and use your Echo Skill when you plan to talk with your parents about a "touchy" subject.

● Remember that your goal is to *talk with*, not *yell at*.

EXERCISE

1. Think of an issue that you'd like to discuss with your parents, but haven't been able to get up the nerve to take to them.
2. List all of the points of discussion you want to bring up.
3. Set up three chairs in your room with two of them facing you, and practice that discussion. Use the tips above, to help you along. Switch to one of the other chairs when you think your mother or father would have something to say, and "answer" yourself.
4. Keep the "talk" going until you have reached a satisfac-

tory ending. Expect the end result to be a compromise, at best.

5. Take that issue to your parents and have a talk, just as you practiced.

6. After the talk, go to your room and evaluate the way it turned out. Did you end up arguing? Which of the above points did you not remember, or not stick to very well? Concentrate on how *you* behaved as you're evaluating the discussion. If the end result is not satisfying or acceptable to you, resolve to take the issue to your parents again in two weeks. In the meantime, take note of what happened this time and how you might change the way you acted, to bring the problem closer to a solution next time.

BEING ANGRY WITH PARENTS

What happened the last time your parents teased you about something that really hit a sore spot, or compared you to a smart, good-looking cousin of yours? How about when you bring home a ninety or ninety-five on an important paper for school, and they ask why you didn't get a hundred?

More than likely, you lost your temper. You started screaming, slammed doors, burst out crying, and generally went into hysterics. And how did they react? Well, they probably didn't take your outburst too seriously.

You *do* have a right to feel anger toward your parents and other authority relationships, and you have a right to express that anger. *But,* you also have a responsibility not to put down or humiliate them in the process.

Your goal in telling someone you are angry, and why, is to *resolve the situation* and take care of the problem at hand—*not* to embarrass or make the other person feel guilty. Follow these hints when you decide to express anger:

1. Be brief. Don't run the point into the ground or drag "old wounds" or unrelated incidents into the discussion. Stick to the issue.
2. Don't accuse, insult, or try to embarrass the person, especially if you are expressing anger toward a parent.
3. Listen to the other person's point of view; there might be a good reason for his or her behavior.
4. If the discussion begins to turn into a fight, end it. Say no more about it; you tried, and a screaming fight will not solve the problem between you.
5. *Never:* (a) threaten to leave or run away; (b) make up a physical sickness "caused" by your anger; (c) carry on the "silent treatment"; (d) cry on purpose; or (e) tell your folks "You don't love me." These are all tricks to try to *manipulate* the other person into *feeling guilty* about making you angry, and are *not* assertive. They also will not solve the problem at hand.
6. If the other person or parent tries to change the subject or make excuses that will not lead to solving the problem, use the Echo Skill, repeating your main point each time you speak.
7. Clouding is useful in arguments, too. Often, when arguing, people will make *judgments* about your behavior, telling you it's wrong, or stupid, or for some reason not what you "should" be doing. Respond *only* to the truth in their accusations—acknowledge what you did or did not do, and tell them why you did it *if* you decide it's appropriate to tell them that—but "cloud over" their judgments about you.
8. When expressing anger toward parents, it's easy to become intimidated, or afraid, because of their authority over you. Respect their authority, but *don't let it stop you from expressing your feelings.* It's helpful here to ask yourself, "How would I handle this anger if I were thirty years old? What are the differences between how I would act then and how I'm acting now?" If those

differences don't make sense to you, try expressing yourself as though you *were* thirty and had been on your own for ten years. In other words, don't be their child—be yourself! (IMPORTANT: If you were an *assertive* thirty-year-old, you would still stop yourself from insulting or putting down your parents, or manipulating them into guilt for making you angry. And you would still steer clear of a fight.)

ANGER SHOULD SOLVE PROBLEMS, NOT CREATE THEM

You just read eight important points to remember when you are expressing anger. The "angry answers" listed below *don't work* in an argument, and should never be used. Can you figure out why they wouldn't work? Read each one, and then, using the spaces provided, briefly explain *why* that answer won't help you.

> *Example:* "There's nothing you can say to change my mind—*nobody* with any sense would do what you just did."

> *Why Not Effective:* Remember the third point—what does "with any sense" mean? Can you judge whether a person "has any sense," when you don't want people to judge *you*? There's a reason for the other person's actions, even though you might not think it's a valid reason.

1. "Well, what about that time you made fun of me in front of that guy? You *knew* you were being crummy."

Why Not Effective:

_____

_____

2. "If you cared at *all* about me, you wouldn't say that."
Why Not Effective: _____

_____

3. "That's just the way I do things. If you don't like it, too
bad." Why Not Effective: _____

_____

4. "Don't tell me you didn't mean to hurt me, I *know* you
did." Why Not Effective: _____

_____

5. "I will *not* 'settle down,' and don't tell me to stop yelling.
I'll yell at you if I want to." Why Not Effective: _____

_____

6. "I can't tell you what I'm upset about, you'll get mad
at me." Why Not Effective: _____

_____

7. (Leaving the room) "I don't want to discuss it." Why
Not Effective: _____

_____

8. "That just shows how ignorant you are sometimes."
Why Not Effective: _____

_____

9. "I'm getting a stomachache from this fight." Why Not
Effective: _____

_____

10. "You're so high-and-mighty, no wonder you don't have any friends." Why Not Effective: _____

_____

Answers

1. Bringing up "old wounds" from the past won't get you closer to solving *today's* problem. Stick to the issue.
2. This is manipulation; you're trying to make the other person feel guilty about his or her behavior, and now you expect to be reassured that you are loved. Sometimes, people say negative things about you because they *do* care—answer only the *truth* in what they say, and "cloud over" the rest.
3. "That's just the way I do things" does not help the other person to *understand* what you do or say. You *don't* have to make excuses for your behavior, but unless you are more tactful (remember, "It seemed right" is always an acceptable explanation), and less belligerent, you can lose friends over small issues.
4. You can't *know* that another person meant to hurt you. Give people a chance. You might say, "I have an idea that you hurt me on purpose. If that's true, I wish you would tell me why, because I can't understand how a person I like a lot would hurt me on purpose." People don't expect such a forthright response, and you'll get a more honest and complete answer than if you fought for hours.
5. We all resent being told to "settle down" when we're fighting, but it's still the best thing to do. Take a deep breath, make yourself comfortable, and start *talking* about the problem at hand.
6. Read point eight again. You have the right to express your feelings to *anyone* who makes you feel angry.

7. Obviously, you won't solve any problems if you won't discuss them.
8. The point in all of these answers is that when you are arguing or angry, you want to respond in a way that will *solve the problem* as quickly, completely, and calmly as possible. Insulting the other person has the opposite effect: Emotions and tempers explode, and instead of settling a conflict you've started a war. Insults hurt people and your goal is to solve a problem, not create new ones.
9. Make-believe illnesses are a cop-out. Running from the argument because you suddenly "got sick" makes it pretty obvious to people that you can't stand the heat. If you're tempted to resort to this kind of "escape" because you've been proven wrong in the argument, it's best to admit it and end the whole matter.
10. This is another insult. If the other person knew how to use the Clouding Skill, how would he or she answer? You've invited an answer such as, "I do have fewer friends than you, but I choose them carefully." At that point, you're no longer on the subject and the problem isn't getting solved. Moral: Insults lead to nowhere.

EXERCISE

1 Pick out two issues that have led to arguments in your family in the past, one for each parent.
2. Set up two chairs in your room, face-to-face, and stage a practice discussion as you did earlier, except that you will be expressing *anger* this time. Keep the above list of pointers with you. When you have resolved one issue to your satisfaction, hold a practice "discussion" with your other parent, using the second issue you chose.
3. Each time you argue with your parents, have an "instant replay" of the argument, as soon as you can get away, alone in your room. Try to figure out how you

could have behaved differently and avoided turning your expression of anger into a fight. You will soon find yourself much more in control of your emotions when you are angry, and much better at getting your point across to the other person—and at solving the problem much quicker!

GOOD MEAL, MOM!

One sure way to convince people that you are ready for some responsibility, as you are learning, is to behave as though you can handle it. This doesn't mean, however, that you should see your family as "people" only when you're trying to resolve a conflict or get what you want.

It's important that they know you are aware of (and appreciate) those times when they go out of their way a little, to make you happy. When you show appreciation, they know that getting ready for adulthood is serious business for you, and not just a temporary, phony trick to get something from them.

Besides the obvious gesture of thanking people, the nicest way to express appreciation is by giving compliments. Compliments should, of course, be given *only* when you feel them sincerely.

When offered as a true, positive expression of the way you feel about a person, or about something he or she has done, compliments go a long way toward deepening and strengthening relationships. People like to hear positive things about themselves, and they don't feel so taken for granted when their work is appreciated. Parents are no exception. Remember, people cannot read your mind, and they won't know that you admire or appreciate them, unless *you* tell them.

EXERCISE

1. For the next three weeks, give *each* member of your family two *sincere* compliments per week.
2. Keep a chart, and write down the compliments you give, so that you will be able to remember the situations at the end of the three weeks. Example:

	Week 1		Week 2		Week 3	
	Comp. 1	Comp. 2	Comp. 1	Comp. 2	Comp. 1	Comp. 2
Mother						
Father						
Brother						
Sister						

3. After three weeks, write a paragraph about your relationship with each member of your family, whether you've noticed any change in the relationship at all (and what it might be), and how you would like the relationship to change further. Add how you felt making the extra effort to be a little nicer and more appreciative toward each of them. Don't feel badly, or be disappointed, if your effort did not change the way your family feels toward you, especially brothers and sisters. Relationships don't change overnight. If they're not used to receiving compliments from you, though, you can be sure they noticed the gesture and might have been a little puzzled by it. Continue giving compliments —*when you feel* the urge to say something nice. Don't create situations when you can make up something positive to say; just don't choke it back when the time is right for a compliment.
4. Suggestion for an assertive birthday, anniversary, or

Christmas present: A night out, with *you* along. Make it an event that the person will enjoy, and go "Dutch" for a bite to eat afterward. This is a nice way of saying "I have fun being with you and like you as a person, even if we *are* in the same family."

HOW WILL THEY REACT?

We have been dealing, in this chapter, mainly with parent–son/daughter relationships and haven't paid much attention to brothers and sisters. This is because most of the problems that keep you from reaching goals at home, and from *becoming less dependent,* are between you and your parents. All of the techniques and exercises, though, can work as well in difficult situations with brothers and sisters. If you need to tell them how you feel about something and aren't sure how to go about it—or you're a little nervous because they might blow up at you—use this chapter.

It's possible that parents and other family members may not welcome your new assertive behavior. You may even be punished for it if you're not very careful and calm about the manner in which you present your honest feelings to them.

The following is a list of ways to make your new assertiveness a little easier for your family to live with. Any *change* in you will, at first, be strange to them, perhaps difficult for them to accept. If you follow these guidelines, however, your family will *not* feel threatened by the "new you." On the contrary, they will be delighted and proud.

1. Understand—and *make it clear to your parents* that you understand—that as long as you depend on your folks financially, you will accept their rules.
2. Remember, and practice every chance you get, *negotia-*

tion without fighting. When fights start, don't participate. Try to make your feelings clear at some other time, when you can convince the other family member(s) to have a talk.

3. Be sure to invite your folks to read this book. At least, talk to them about your efforts to become a more honest, direct, and assertive person. *Don't defy them* with your assertiveness; ask them to play an active part in your growth.
4. You can help your parents to become more assertive in their relationships, too—but *without* interfering. If you hear your mother speak of a friend who continually takes advantage of her, for instance, you could go over your Rights and Skills, as a quick review. Then, say to your mother, "You know, I'll bet if you told her such and such [depending on the situation], that would stop her, because you have a right . . ."
5. Regularly—as often as you feel it, in fact—express affection toward each member of your family.
6. If your folks don't look at your assertiveness favorably, do things and go places with them more often. If you feel strange asking them to go to a show with you, try pretending that they are your cousins, only five years older than you, and enjoy their company.
7. Try to introduce your parents to a new craft or hobby you've discovered. *Don't* force it on them if they show no interest, but if you think they might go for the idea, suggest that you take a class in it, *together.*
8. Most important, whenever something nice happens to you as a result of your new assertive behavior, *share* the experience with your family! Tell them how you had acted in that particular situation in the past, what you did differently this time, and how your behavior changed things for the better. They will be happy to

learn of the ways in which assertiveness is making your life more satisfying, and by your letting them in on the experience, they will become *more supportive* of your efforts to be more effective.

4.

It's Your Body

Looks are pretty important. It's not much comfort to hear that five years from now, the opposite sex will be attracted to you for your personality. Now the most popular people around you seem to be the best-looking ones—and five years is too long to wait.

It will be a nice surprise to you, then, to discover that as you behave more assertively, you get what you want from your relationships because of who you are and *how you act,* and *not* because of the way you look. A big nose, an overbite, or a complexion that looks as though the navy used it for target practice will never stop you from being an *effective person*—one whom other people listen to. No matter how you look, if you are a person who deals honestly and kindly and directly in all of your relationships, you will always have friends.

Still, we all feel sometimes that we were cheated in the "looks department," one way or another. When we are teased about one of our physical features it makes matters worse because we feel we are being judged as people on that basis.

Every person who reads this book looks a little better than some people, and a little worse than others. If you are an assertive person, it's no big deal—you already *trust your values*. You like yourself because you *behave* in a way that makes you *feel good* about the things you say and do in your relationships. In fact, since assertive people do all they can to make their lives satisfying (instead of waiting for someone else to step in and do it), they figure that they look just fine.

We are stuck with our basic features, and we sort of build around those to construct a certain *image*. That image, though, shouldn't be molded according to what we think other people might like. An image tells people who we are, the kind of lives we lead, how comfortable we like to be. With the use of clothes, comb, and cosmetics, we *look the way we want to look,* without depending on the approval of other people, or even asking if it's "all right," or worrying if our friends are looking the same way. Our looks are effective *only* if they are an extension of *what we are.*

This doesn't mean wearing jeans to an aunt's funeral, or an evening gown or tuxedo to church, just because you feel like it. Such attention-getting devices are anything but assertive. In fact, they let people know that you are insecure about yourself and have to resort to obnoxious tricks to get others to notice you.

Looking the way you want to means that you have evaluated yourself and changed those things that you can change, *if* they stop you from being the person you want to be. If you'd like to improve your tennis game but are out of breath after ten minutes, a little dieting and jogging could build up your endurance. If it irritates you to see the world through a set of frames, you might use the cash from your part-time job for a set of contact lenses.

These are cases in which the way you look: (1) gets in your way; and (2) can, with a little effort, be changed.

You are correcting a problem. If, however, you jog because your friend Jeannie jogs and people pay attention to her when she talks about it, you are not being assertive if you take up jogging. You're doing it because Jeannie does and it seems to make her more popular.

Are there things about yourself that you'd like to change because it would make you feel better about yourself—or more effective—if you did? Let's find out.

BODY INVENTORY

1. Stand nude in front of a full-length mirror, with a chart like the one below.
2. Starting at the top of your head, evaluate every single part of your body—eyes, hair, fingers—everything. Don't skip over anything. Fill in the chart below, indicating whether you would like to change some parts of your appearance, if they can be changed, and *why*.
3. When you have finished evaluating your body, look at the reasons why you want to change some aspects of the way you look. Are the reasons basically to make you feel better about yourself, or are they to impress someone else? Cross out those things you would change to impress other people, shrug your shoulders, and make a mental promise to yourself that you just won't let those things bother you too much. You will need that energy to concentrate on making changes that will improve *your* situation.
4. Plan to change those features you chose—the ones that *can* be changed and will make you happier by doing so. Start with any one you wish.
5. If the changes you want to make involve disciplining yourself, such as exercising or altering your eating habits, it's best not to try too much at once. Attack those problems one at a time, and let yourself enjoy each new

accomplishment for a week or so before you go on to the next.

Feature	OK with Me? (Yes, No)	If No, Can It Be Changed?	Reason for Wanting Change
Hairstyle			
Eyes—Glasses			
Eyes—Makeup		.	
(etc.)			

EXERCISE

For one week, carry a small notebook with you. Every time you feel badly about your physical appearance, or wish you had hair or skin (or anything) as nice as someone else's, write it down. At the end of the week, look at all of the negative reactions to yourself. If you're like most people, you'll see that you've been spending a lot of time comparing yourself to other people, instead of enjoying and using your own good qualities.

WAS THAT A PUT-DOWN?

When someone insults you or makes fun of you, it's because they lack the courage to deal with you directly. They're afraid to say what it is about your *behavior* that *really* bothers them.

That fact gives little comfort if someone hurts your feelings. We aren't referring to honest criticism here, but cruelty. Since most mean insults are put-downs of one's physical appearance, let's talk about nasty people a little here. Insulters resort to put-downs—which are really cop-outs—because they aren't confident enough of their own qualities to deal with the real conflict between you.

You have every right to feel as though you're "one-up"

on those people, because you *do* have the strength to be direct about your feelings, and they do not. They are afraid to put the *real* cards on the table, and though they may get a lot of attention and are usually surrounded by a lot of people, it's pretty hard to love a person who behaves in such an obviously cowardly (and irritating) way, and they can't have many real friends. These hints will help you to deal with the mean insulters in your crowd:

1. You do not have to be a friend to them, and don't let anyone tell you that you "should" be. Perhaps you have to be around those people, at school and social activities, and it's not a good idea to stay home when something's going on, just to avoid being exposed to certain people. That would only prove that you, too, are having a hard time facing up to the unpleasant situation. However, you are *not* obligated to invest your time and affection in people who are *bad for you,* who cause you to feel hurt, and who take away from you. Don't be mean back at them—just don't make them a part of your life any more than you have to. If parents or others ask you why you no longer spend time with so-and-so, and if you feel like giving an answer (though none is necessary), simply say that he or she is always nasty to you, and you see no point in continuing that kind of relationship.

2. When you are insulted, never begin your reply with the words *I* or *because.* You will sound as though you are defending yourself or apologizing for being the way you are.

3. Don't blurt out the first thing that comes to your mind when you are insulted. Stop for a moment to think, and take a deep breath before you answer.

4. No one who insults you is "innocent" or "doesn't realize what he or she is saying." If this is the case, *it's time they learned.* Don't be afraid to embarrass such people by saying, "Don't you realize that you can hurt some-

one's feelings, talking like that?" or, "Why is it that whenever you don't know what to say, you say something nasty? What are you afraid of, anyway?"

5. Keep one or two such phrases in stock, so that you can use them in any insulting situation when you're at a loss for words. A simple "Was that a put-down?" or, "What is it that *really* bothers you about me?" will catch them off guard (they expect you to be defensive) and usually works just fine.

EXERCISE: WRITE DOWN YOUR PUT-DOWNS

For one week, keep an "Insult Journal," and record every time someone insults you—*and* each time you insult another person. Here are two examples of entries for your journal:

Insults by Me

Day	Whom I Insulted	What I Said
Monday	My sister Anna	"You look like a big sausage poured into those pants."

Insults to Me

Day	Who Said It	What He/She Said
Thursday	Derek, school-mate	"Those shoes have been out of style for two years."

How I Answered
"Why don't you take a flying leap?"

1. After a week, look at those insults directed at you. Was there any truth in the things that were said? How could you have used your Clouding Skill to respond to the insults? This is a good collection of real-life situations, which acutally happened to you, to use for sharpening your Clouding.

   How did you respond to the put-downs? The answer to Derek's put-down only let him know that he accomplished his purpose—he made you mad. It would have been much more effective to say "Yes, they have," and keep walking.

2. For each insult you received, think of a different answer that would utilize your Clouding Skill, and write it down. Alone in your room, "replay" the incidents, using your new answers. You will find that the next time you are insulted by the same people, it will be easier to deal with just the *truth* in what they say, without getting hurt or upset.

   If Clouding doesn't give you an answer that satisfies you, don't be afraid to embarrass such a person and use "stock" answers. Those phrases call attention to what insulters are doing—that is, putting you down— and using them in front of other people will embarrass the nasty one, and he or she will be off your back soon.

3. Look at the entries for the times you put other people down. Were the insults necessary? Usually, you can get your point across more effectively if you simply state the facts, without insulting. For instance, telling your sister Anna that she looks like a sausage will not only hurt her feelings, but she'll probably also feel a little stubborn, and won't change her pants. So, what was accomplished?

   She would probably, though, appreciate your telling her, in a straightforward, nonjudging way, that those pants are much too tight. Suggest that if she wears them, the first thing people will see is the weight she has gained, and another pair would look a lot nicer.

4. Read each insult you gave to ther people, and think of another way to get across the *truth* in your statement, without embarrassing anyone. In other words, "cloud over" your own insults! This will not only help you to convey the truth to people more effectively, but also give you more practice in Clouding, for when you're on the receiving end!

BODY TALK

No matter what pearls of wisdom you are laying on someone, or on a group of people, you won't be very convincing if your body isn't behaving as assertively as your words are put together. The *way you express* your feelings is as important as what you say. There are a lot of points to remember in controlling your body as you speak, especially if you are upset or nervous, and it's difficult to keep each of the following racing through your head at the right time. It is possible, though, to accomplish assertive delivery if you practice these and remember *comfort* just before you enter into an uncomfortable situation. Try to assume a "centered" body posture, and don't try to distort what comes naturally—making your voice more "breathy" than usual, or louder. Calmness and evenness in your delivery are more effective than put-on tricks that will only distract from what you are saying.

Expressing yourself effectively can be easily mastered, with a little practice, if you keep in mind your level of anxiety, verbal content, and delivery.

Anxiety

Eye contact. If you want to play some sort of flirting game as you talk with someone, look away from them as you speak. But, if you want them to listen to what you're saying, the best way to keep their attention is to look them directly in the eye. When you can keep steady eye contact with a person, he or she knows that you are confident and in control of the situation; when your eyes wander, you are avoiding the other person, and he or she notices it. It's much easier to maintain eye contact when you are listening than when you are speaking, but it's important that you appear equally relaxed when doing both.

Relaxed posture. An appearance of a relaxed, comfortable position of your body gives another image of control over the situation. A rigid body, when every small movement is a conscious effort, is an obvious clue to your anxiety. Being too slouched, on the other hand, gives the impression that you are not interested.

Nervous joking. Nervous laughter or joking is a cover-up for your discomfort and tells the other person that you either don't know what to say or don't want to say it. But it doesn't help you to express your true feelings; it could give the impression that you don't take this matter very seriously. If you find yourself beginning to laugh because you're nervous, it's much more effective to come right out and say, "Look, it's a little difficult for me to say these things, but they *are* important to me, so give me a minute to put these thoughts into the right words."

Excessive movements. Let your arm and hand gestures be natural. Unnecessary and excessive movements distract the other person's attention from what you're saying. Also, let your movements be consistent with your words—don't smile when you are expressing anger, for instance.

Verbal Content

Say what you mean to say. If you are dissatisfied with someone's behavior, say that you are, and why. Don't tell a friend, "I sure do seem to be loaded down with a lot of extra work lately," when what you really mean is, "It annoys me that you ask me to help you with your homework so often, because it cuts into my free time too much and I think you ought to depend on *you* to pass this course, not on me."

Be specific. If you beat around the bush, that increases the possibility that others will misinterpret what you are saying. If a friend asks your honest opinion of a project he put together for art class, and your first impression is that it was thrown together at the last minute, say exactly that.

Don't apologize. If you need to ask a favor of someone, don't make excuses or apologize for the circumstances that led to your need to ask. Be direct, say that you need this favor, and ask if it would be possible for him or her to do it. Apologizing and making excuses tends to weaken the impact of your message, and the other person might not understand that what you are saying, whether you are asking a favor or expressing irritation, is important to you.

Delivery

Speak almost immediately. When you are being criticized or are in another awkward situation, take a deep breath (just long enough to figure out what you really mean to say), and then say it. This tells people that you are sure of yourself and of your point of view.

Tone. Watch the tone of your voice. I once met a very talented woman at a large, week-long conference, but I was the only person out of two hundred who discovered her talent. It was by accident; she was alone in her room, playing guitar and singing beautifully. When she was around people, though, she spoke so softly that you actually had to put your face against hers in order to hear what she was whispering about, and it was just too much bother. On the other hand, a very loud or "whiny" voice is irritating, and people tend to avoid listening to you if you make it difficult for them to do so, one way or another. An assertive delivery alone, of course, won't guarantee favorable consequences or ensure that you'll get what you want out of your relationships with people. It does, however, *increase your chances* when you can get people to listen to what you are saying.

When you know that you are going to be in a difficult situation, you can practice your end of it alone and plan what you will want to say. When you run through it alone first, it makes it a little easier to transfer your feelings in real life.

EXERCISE

Make up three mildly difficult situations. One of them will be asking a favor of someone, one will be criticizing someone whose behavior annoys you, and the last will be a request you know is coming and have good reason to turn down.

Using the above ways in which you can express yourself more effectively, and keeping your Rights and Skills handy, practice those conversations alone in your room. Anticipate the reactions the other person might have, and have your responses ready. Keep practicing each until you feel confident that you'll be able to deliver your message effectively.

Take your planned situations out into the open and use them with those individuals. When you are finished, write down your feelings about your behavior—did you maintain good eye contact and keep other anxiety indicators under control? How about your posture and voice? Did you stammer or whine, or were you able to get your point across naturally? Make a note of what you think were weaknesses in the way you expressed yourself, for each situation.

After you have looked over the notes you took and decided how you could have delivered your message more effectively, repeat the entire exercise. Think of three new situations, changing the people involved if appropriate, and practice the conversations alone beforehand. Make a new set of notes after each talk, and compare them with the notes from the first time you did the exercise. You should see an improvement in your assertive expression of feelings. If there are still aspects of your expression you would like to strengthen, repeat the exercise again. Most of us come into enough contact with asking or denying favors, or criticism, in our daily lives that you'll get plenty of practice without creating more situations on your own.

RELAX YOURSELF!

You cannot be both tense and relaxed at the same time. It's difficult to assert yourself if you are not physically relaxed, even if you're *not* in an awkward situation. When you are feeling uptight, it's hard to concentrate on studies or even to enjoy yourself when you're supposed to be relaxing!

Daily living is a lot more enjoyable if we're not full of tension all of the time. When difficult situations do arise, they are easier to cope with if our bodies are relaxed. More important, if relaxation—erasing stress and anxiety—is practiced, it can become so much a part of us that when anxiety situations do come up, it will be *natural* and automatic to feel relaxed, and we can concentrate on the message we are trying to get across, rather than the *way we come across* to the other person.

EXERCISE

This muscle relaxation exercise * is a popular one, and many people practice it regularly every day, just because it feels good. It's also a good way to begin to prepare yourself for difficult situations, whether they involve confrontations with other people, exams in school, or having to speak in front of a group of people.

Before you begin, lie on your bed for five minutes, with the lights out. Imagine that you are in a wonderful place—on a beach, maybe, or at the edge of a mountain stream. Try to "hear" the sounds that would be happening around you, and "smell" the fragrances. Enjoy being there for a few minutes, then begin the following steps, in this order:

1. Tense the muscles in your right hand by making a tight fist. Hold it for five seconds, then relax for half a minute. Repeat this (and any other step) if that part of your body doesn't feel *completely* relaxed.
2. Tense the muscles in your right upper arm by bending your arm and making a "muscle." Hold the tension for five seconds, then relax for half a minute.
3. Tense the muscles in your left hand by making a fist, hold for five seconds, then relax for half a minute.
4. Tense the muscles in your left upper arm by making a muscle, hold for five seconds, then relax for half a minute.
5. Tense the muscles in your forehead by frowning, as hard as you can, for five seconds, and relax for half a minute.
6. Tense the muscles in your eyes by closing them as

* From E. Jacobsen, *Progressive Relaxation,* Chicago: University of Chicago Press, 1938.

tightly as you can. Hold for five seconds, then relax for half a minute.

7. Tense the muscles in your nose by wrinkling it hard for five seconds; relax for half a minute.
8. Press your lips together tightly and force your tongue against the roof of your mouth, as hard as you can, for five seconds. Relax for half a minute.
9. Tense your jaw by clenching your teeth together for five seconds, then relax for half a minute.
10. Try to look directly "above" you as you're lying, stretching your neck as hard as you can, for five seconds. Relax for half a minute.
11. Tense your shoulders and upper back by shrugging your shoulders tightly for five seconds, and relax for half a minute.
12. Tense your back by arching it, as hard as you can while still lying down, for five seconds. Relax for half a minute.
13. Tense your chest by taking a deep breath and holding it for ten seconds, then relax for half a minute.
14. Pull your abdomen in as tightly as you can and hold it for ten seconds, then relax for half a minute.
15. Press your heels into the bed or floor as hard as you can. Hold for five seconds, then relax for half a minute.
16. Tense your ankles and calves by pointing them away from your body, as far as you can. Hold for five seconds, and relax for half a minute.

After you have completed all sixteen steps, remain lying down for ten minutes. Don't concentrate on anything in particular, just daydream. At the end of the ten minutes, *plan* to come back to alertness by having a "countdown"; tell yourself that in thirty seconds you will be finished with your relaxation exercise and will get up and go about your business.

Do the Jacobsen Relaxation Exercise every day for

one week. Combined with believing in your Rights and putting your Skills into practice, you will find that feeling physically relaxed actually does make a difference in your behavior, and in your effectiveness as a person. Try to continue using the relaxation exercise at least twice a week, to keep stress and anxiety where they belong—in the background.

5.

Friendship: The Necessary Refreshment

We can try to get by without friends, but no matter how hard it is to deal with people sometimes, it's nothing compared to dealing without them. Being loved by good friends warms our lives and brings a sense of peace in even the worst crisis.

A few chapters back, you read that assertiveness is a skill that must first be learned, then practiced all of the time, in order to keep it sharp—like typing or dribbling a basketball.

Being a good friend—and, in turn, *having* good friends—works the same way. It's not automatic. This chapter is packed with exercises that will help you to recognize, communicate with, and become closer to the friends in your life. As you go through each section, you will be working toward one goal: to be a *good friend.*

If you are a good friend to have, you can make these two important statements about *every* friendship in your life:

I accept my friend. (I don't expect my friend to be any different, in any way, than he or she already is.)

I am honest with my friend. (My friend *always* knows where he or she stands with me. Sometimes I have to figure out a way to say something without hurting anyone's feelings, but I always say the truth.)

If you have friends about whom you *cannot* say these two things, they are not true friends with you, no matter how long you've known each other or how much you hang out together. Wanting someone to be *different* than he or she is means that you love the person *you think he or she ought to be,* not the person who already is.

When this happens, you could fall into the trap of trying to *manipulate* your friend into changing. Manipulation and true friendship *cannot* exist at the same time. While you are reading this book to learn how to assert your rights and become a more effective person, you can't take away other people's right to be effective *in their own way,* any more than they can do that to you!

Honesty is just as important as acceptance. If you have a friend who constantly does things to irritate you—mooches, cuts into lines ahead of you, puts down other friends of yours—and you never let your friend know how you feel, his or her irritating behavior will go on. On the other hand, expressing affection or gratitude to a friend when you really feel it will *reinforce* (support) that friend's good behavior. It will let him or her know that if he or she acts in that way, the consequences (results) are satisfying to both of you, and your friendship will keep growing.

SPIT IT OUT

Communicating with friends and other equal relationships is extra-hard sometimes—since you have more freedom to *control* those relationships, you also have more *responsibility.* You have to say more and do more to keep the friendship going. If you don't say things in a way that will get your point across the way you want, you can end up forfeiting or giving up *your* half of the control to the other person.

EXERCISE

In this exercise, we will use your *own* behavior as an example in learning to be *specific* in expressing yourself. Once you can be specific about what *you* do, and how you feel about it, it will be natural to use your skills to express your feelings about the things other people do. More simply, you are going to practice saying precisely what you mean.

The two examples below are very *vague* statements a person might make about his or her behavior. Each is followed by a very *specific* statement that obviously gets to the root of the problem—and, therefore, the solution—much more quickly and completely.

Vague: I'm always mad at my sister; we just can't get along.

Specific: My sister criticizes everything I do. I feel mad and embarrassed around her all the time, because I know more digs are always coming. I get too flustered to be calm when it happens. I've never told her that she hurts my feelings and that I'd like her to give us a chance to be friends.

Vague: I get nervous around my friend Nick whenever we're together.

Specific: Nick is constantly tapping his fingers on a table. Tappity-tap, tappity-tap, all the time. It's just a nervous habit, but I can't even concentrate on what other people around us are saying. I like Nick, but this makes me want to stay away from him. I've yelled at him to stop it when I finally can't stand it anymore, but I've never told him, seriously and calmly, that it's really getting in the way of our otherwise good friendship. He doesn't even realize why I'm always grouchy around him. I ought to tell him how I feel, so we can start having fun together again. [What we're looking at here, remember, is *your* behavior—expressing your feelings in the most effective way possible—not Nick's. The tapping may or may not stop.]

EXERCISE

Write down five experiences or feelings about *your* behavior around friends. Do it as in the examples above—first in very vague terms, then more specifically, putting down exactly *what it is* about the way *you act* with those friends that bothers you. If you have trouble coming up with the specifics—in other words, if you know you feel uncomfortable when you interact with a friend but can't quite figure out *why*—you may not be keeping your Rights and Skills in mind, only your anxiety. If this is the case, look over chapter two again, and figure out which Rights are being stepped on—or which Skills you're not using.

Keep your list for a week. During that week, try to express the way you feel to your friends—in very *specific* terms—whenever you are with them. (You can use the same friend for more than one situation.) After you are with those friends again, come back to your list and answer the following questions for each situation.

Look at your answers. In each case, if you're still not satisfied with the way the friendship is going, examine your answers to the last three questions and plan to tackle the problem again. Be persistent. Keep at it until you and your friend have reached a solution you can both live with comfortably.

	1	2	3	4	5
Did I feel the same old discomfort with my friend?					
Did I express my feelings?					
How was my "body language"?					
Did I specifically say what I meant to say and why I felt the way I did?					
What was my friend's reaction?					
Do I feel we began to solve the problem?					
Do I think we need to talk about it further or work on it a little more? In what way?					
Am I satisfied with the way I handled myself? If not, what should I do differently next time?					

THE WORD IS NEGOTIATION

Expressing your feelings is the first step toward *negotiation,* and it's the best way to work out both major and minor problems with friends—or, for that matter, with all relationships.

When you are having a serious conflict with a friend, there are three things you can do. One, you can knuckle under, give in, and forget that you have any rights at all. Two, you can have a fight. Or, three, you can take the trouble to *negotiate—compromise—*and get the problem out of the way, so that you can enjoy being with your friend again.

In negotiating, there are three main steps to follow: (1) expressing your feelings; (2) specifying why you feel the way you do (as you did in the above exercise); and (3) outlining the *consequences* of the *other* person's behavior.

You've already practiced specifically expressing *your* feelings. Now we're going to take it one step further and learn how to deal with the behavior of *others*.

Let's go back to Nick, the tappity-tap guy. In the above section, we were concentrating on expressing *our* feelings, without worrying too much about what Nick's reaction would be or outlining the consequences. You could begin to negotiate the problem with Nick in this way:

Express feelings:	Nick, your tapping is irritating me . . .
Be specific:	. . . because it distracts from what we're all talking about.
Consequences (bad):	If you don't stop, I'm going to quit hanging around you, because I really can't stand it.
Consequences (good):	If you stop, it's going to be a lot more fun for me to go places with you.

Obviously, outlining the *good* consequences of Nick's change (stopping the tappity-tap business) will make him *want to stop* more than threatening him. It's easier to catch a fly with honey.

It's important to note here that you are *not* manipulating Nick into changing himself, just to please you. What you are doing is honestly telling him about something that gets in the way of your friendship, and how much better things would be if the problem were dealt with. He may not even realize he's tapping, let alone making you uncomfortable. Remember Right No. 4, "You have the right to say, 'I don't know,' or 'I don't understand!'" Well, Nick has the same right—you can't expect him to be able to read your mind and know how you feel. You have to tell him.

EXERCISE

Five irritating experiences are listed below. For each one, using the three steps of negotiation, write down what you could say to the culprit to negotiate a solution.

At the end of the exercise are five possible solutions. When you are finished, compare your answers to the ones in the book, and decide if your negotiations would be as effective, or even better. If you are using this book in a class or assertiveness workshop, compare your answers to those of your classmates, and see how many ways one situation can be negotiated. Or, invite a friend to do the exercise, and check the two sets of answers against each other. When you see how different your answers are, you'll also see that negotiation is an open-ended process—every problem has a dozen possible solutions, some better than others, and sometimes finding the best one calls for a little imagination!

1. You have a lot in common with your friend Jackie, and she's fun to be with, except for one thing. She gives very detailed, moment-by-moment instructions for every little thing you do while you're with her. She tells you how you should be sitting to avoid a sore back, what you should say to the clerk in the store, how slowly you should be chewing your food. It's worse than hanging around with a teacher. You've decided to tell Jackie how much she bugs you.

Express feelings:

Be specific:

Consequences (bad):

Consequences (good):

2. You're on a big diet, and you've already lost ten pounds. The last five will be the hardest, and you're really into going all the way and losing them. At a party, though, the hostess keeps pestering you to eat more pizza. You're having a hard enough time resisting, and you wish she'd just leave you alone. You've got to get her off your back about food.

Express feelings:

Be specific:

Consequences (bad):

Consequences (good):

3. Joe really admires your math abilities. He tells people what a whiz you are and how much you help him. The trouble is, you're sick of helping him—he doesn't even try to figure out his own answers anymore. He just gave you his usual, sweet request: "You're so much better at this than me—why don't you see what you can do with this problem? I don't know where to begin." This time, you'll tell him how you feel.

Express feelings:

Be specific:

Consequences (bad):

Consequences (good):

4. For the third time in a row, Jerry, your neighbor, has pooped out on you. First, he backed out when he said

he'd help you move some heavy furniture in your room. Then, he overslept when you planned to go to a baseball game with him. This time it was really important— he was going to drive you to pick up the cake for your parents' anniversary party. You'll have someone else pick up the cake in plenty of time, but Jerry has to be told that he can't expect people to put up with his never coming through.

Express feelings: _____

Be specific: _____

Consequences (bad): _____

Consequences (good): _____

5. You've been Lisa's friend for a long time. There are no real problems in your relationship—you're used to each other's habits, you can disagree without being afraid it will hurt your friendship, and you share intimate feelings you'd never tell anyone else. At a party last week, though, Lisa was with a guy who looked older than most of your friends, and you saw her pop some sort of a pill. You've never tried to tell each other what to do, but you're plenty worried. You've got to say something about it.

Express feelings: _____

Be specific: _____

Consequences (bad): _____

Consequences (good): _____

SOME POSSIBLE NEGOTIATIONS

1. Jackie, the would-be teacher.

Express feelings: Jackie, I can't stand your endless instructions anymore . . .

Be specific:	. . . because I resent your thinking I need to be told how to do the simplest things, as if I were five years old.
Consequences (bad):	If you don't stop it, I'm going to start treating *you* like an idiot in front of people, and see how you like it.
Consequences (good):	You know, if you'd stop trying to be such an authority all of the time, I could enjoy being with you, instead of dreading it.

2. The pizza pusher.

Express feelings:	I'd like you to quit coaxing me to eat . . .
Be specific:	. . . because I've done a great job on my diet, and I want to be in shape this summer.
Consequences (bad):	If you don't shut up about that pizza, you're going to be wearing it in a minute.
Consequences (good):	If you don't tempt me with pizza anymore, I'll forget about food and have a better time at your party.

3. Joe, the math moocher.

Express feelings:	Joe, I'm tired of doing your homework for you . . .
Be specific:	. . . because you're not learning anything, and I'm feeling that you take advantage of me. First you flatter me, then you put me to work. I don't like it.

Consequences (bad):	If you don't stop, we'll just have to stop being friends, because right now our entire friendship is your sweet talk and my work, and it's going to stop.
Consequences (good):	If you cut out the phony sweet talk, I'll show you how to do this problem, and you'll know how to do it yourself next time.

4. Jerry, the lazy neighbor.

Express feelings:	Jerry, I'm really fed up with never being able to depend on you . . .
Be specific:	. . . because you really leave people out in the cold. This was an important errand, and there were a lot of people, not just me, counting on you to get that cake.
Consequences (bad):	This was the last straw. Since you can't do any better than dump on people all of the time, I'm dumping on you. Don't come back until you grow up a little.
Consequences (good):	You have a reputation now for being lazy and irresponsible. I like you, but I know better than to count on you for anything, and now my whole family feels the same way. Maybe if you'd make an effort to follow through on things you say you'll do, we'll change our minds and feel better about you.

5. Lisa the pill-popper.

Express feelings:	Look, Lisa, I'm really worried about what I saw at that party . . .
Be specific:	. . . because that guy looked like a real creep. He was too old to be partying around us, and anybody who would go around giving out pills is bad news. He wouldn't even talk to any of our friends, and I think he's trouble.
Consequences (bad):	I'm worried enough about you to go to your parents. If you won't shape yourself up, we'll have to do it for you.
Consequences (good):	That guy can go to jail for a long time for what he does; does that sound exciting to you? Tell me where you're coming from on this, because I don't understand why you're fooling around with this strange stuff. Let's talk about it, and maybe we'll both understand things a little better.

FRIENDS IN NEED

If you're with a friend and feel that you *don't* control a full 50 percent of what goes on in that friendship, you know you're being manipulated.

Nothing is more irritating than friends who try to manipulate us. In the last exercise, four of the five questions were situations in which we all find ourselves—being stepped on, or used, and a little helpless around a strong, pushy person.

We've learned how to make our feelings known when we're in conflict with a friend. Now we can look at our overall behavior when someone tries to walk on us, and evaluate how effectively we react to the entire situation.

Read the list of reactions below. These are all things you *should* do, when you feel that someone is pushing you around, in order to handle the conflict assertively. Put an X next to those you honestly think you do, and score yourself when you're finished. Give yourself five points for each thing you almost always do, three points for each thing you do about half of the time, and one point for each thing you almost never do.

When I feel I'm being manipulated or stepped on, I:

_____ tell the other person my specific complaint.

_____ stop for a moment and decide what would be the best thing to do, before I blurt out something I'll be sorry I said.

_____ consciously weigh the alternatives—and the consequences of each—that I could take, as I'm talking.

_____ give the other person a chance to explain.

_____ express my feelings without blaming or putting down the other person.

_____ don't accuse the other person of having secret, nasty motives.

_____ try to reach a solution, not make a fight.

_____ express concern as to the effects of these lousy circumstances on the *other* person's situation, and the effects on our friendship, instead of only talking about how *I'm* affected.

_____ am brief and to the point.

_____ am firm in my position.

_____ admit I'm wrong or too critical of the other person, if our discussion works out that way and if it's the truth.

_____ look the other person directly in the eye as I talk.

_____ play no manipulation tricks, or try to make my friend feel guilty for making me angry.

_____ control my gestures and voice—tone, loudness.

Add up your points. The highest score you can get is 70. How did you rate?

50–70 points. You handle other people's manipulation pretty well. With this score, you've pretty much mastered the Skills needed for asserting your Rights. If you answered honestly, you apparently practice those Skills, too. Keep practicing.

30–50 points. You're trying to solve conflicts reasonably, but you're probably still backing down when the other person is extra-pushy. Read your Rights and Skills again, get yourself revved up, and redo the exercises at the end of chapter two. Also, go over the sections in chapter four on assertive body language. It's a lot easier to assert your Rights when the rest of your body is expressing the same feelings as your words.

Under 30 points. This is a good time for you to decide *not* to skip a single exercise in this book. If your score was under 30, you haven't been using your Skills nearly enough to be effective when your Rights are threatened by a person who manipulates. Reread the Rights and Skills section (chapter two), and do all of the exercises that follow it. Then, go back through the entire book and pick up every exercise you missed. Practicing your assertiveness Skills will get easier each time you do it—*beginning* with the first time!

A LITTLE RESPECT

What makes honesty and acceptance so essential in a true friendship is that they add up to *respect.*

Respect is a pretty vague concept, though. If a friend would ask you, "I know we have fun together, but do you *respect* me?" you would probably answer, "Of course I do," without thinking much about it.

It's difficult sometimes to sort out true friends from people with whom you just spend time. In the final tally, people have to fall into one of two categories: those who are bad for you and those who are good for you. The one deciding factor in determining that is *mutual respect*— you and your friend must *both* respect each other, or the friendship isn't real.

No one can be a perfect friend all of the time, but the following exercise can help you to find out if you respect your friends, how much they respect you, and which relationships need work.

EXERCISE

First, we'll work on *your* feelings. Begin by listing the four people whom you consider to be your best, closest friends. They don't have to be the ones with whom you spend the most *time;* it's more important that they are the four people to whom you feel *closer* than anyone else— even if they live in another city.

Now, answer yes or no to the ten questions below, about your feelings and behavior toward *each* of them. You can use the list and chart that follow for your answers.

1. Do you generally support your friend as a person, even if you disagree, without putting him or her down?
2. Do you *work* at sharing thoughts and feelings with your friend?
3. Do you treat your friend as an individual, instead of just hanging around him or her so you'll have a friend to be with? In other words, do you avoid "using" your friend?
4. Do you avoid judging your friend, and accept that he or she does some things because they work best, even if they are very different from what you do?

5. Do you sincerely try to understand where your friend is coming from when you disagree?
6. Do you make positive, supportive comments about the things your friend does, as well as honest criticism?
7. Do you express affection for your friend?
8. Are you "there" when your friend needs you, even if it's not convenient sometimes?
9. Do you avoid trying to manipulate or control your friend?
10. Do you enjoy doing nice things for your friend?

GIVING RESPECT

	Friend 1	Friend 2	Friend 3	Friend 4
1. Support				
2. Express feelings				
3. Use				
4. Judging				
5. Understand				
6. Feedback				
7. Affection				
8. There				
9. Don't manipulate				
10. Do things				

Look at your answers—how respectful are you toward your close friends?

Keep this chart, and answer the same questions again —using the same four friendships—in two weeks. In the meantime, concentrate on your no answers, and try to change them to yeses before the two weeks are up.

Now, using the chart below, evaluate how much respect those same four friends give to *you*. Are they supportive, and accepting, and up-front with you most of the time? Answer the same ten questions about their respectful behavior that you answered about your own. Fill in the chart with yes or no for each friend.

GETTING RESPECT

	Friend 1	Friend 2	Friend 3	Friend 4
1. Support				
2. Express feelings				
3. Use				
4. Judging				
5. Understand				
6. Feedback				
7. Affection				
8. There				
9. Don't manipulate				
10. Do things				

How do your friends rate at giving respect to you? If the friendships are real, most of the squares should contain a yes.

The last step in this exercise is the hardest. Using the negotiating skills you learned earlier, go to each friend and let him or her know that you are bothered by the treatment you're getting, what specifically bothers you, and what the consequences will be if some changes *are* made. Here's an example:

Express feelings:	You know, it bothers me that we've never really said how much we like each other . . .
Be specific:	. . . because I really do appreciate the kind of friend you are, and I know you feel the same way. I think it's good to let people know when you like them a lot—it feels good for me to say it, and it would feel good to hear it, too.
Consequences (good):	Maybe if we make an effort to say, "I like you, being your friend is a terrific thing for me," a little more often, we'll have an easier time when we don't agree on things, too. Anyway, *I'm* glad we're friends. How do you feel about it?

Don't be discouraged if your friends are surprised or a little embarrassed at your asking for more respect—or if they don't return the respect you're offering. They may never become as assertive as you. If the friendship is important to you, keep trying. When people aren't used to communicating effectively, they can't be expected to open up overnight. Eventually, if they care about the relationship at all, they'll begin talking about their feelings and behavior toward you—with a little coaxing from you, of course.

HOW TO BE A PROFESSIONAL BORE

It amazes me that some people—regardless of how much they read or learn about how to be assertive—continue to be such expert bores that almost everyone hates to see them coming. It seems impossible to know about assertiveness and continue to carry a down bag. But some people work very hard at it, and they do a good job.

If you're one of those folks who sincerely wants to be boring, no matter how much people around you are growing, follow these ten easy hints. If you follow these carefully, I guarantee you'll be the most boring, mishy-mashy wimp in your crowd.

1. Tell someone you're horny.
2. Gush.
3. Be the kind of person who's too lazy to pick up a dictionary and look up *gush* if you don't understand what it means.
4. Begin sentences with phrases like, "I'm sorry to bother you again, but . . ."
5. Analyze someone else's motives for what he or she does.
6. Gossip.
7. Talk about something you've talked about twice in the last week, to anyone.
8. Talk for more than one minute about either your diet or how tired you are.
9. Complain that you have nothing to do.
10. Put yourself down.

If, on the other hand, you'd rather be *interesting* than boring, try this trick to be aware of the boring things you say or do.

Copy the list above on a piece of paper, and carry it around with you for one week. Keep track of *every* time you do something on this list, by marking it with a check mark (✓).

At the end of each day, count the number of checks— or boring things you did—for that day. Before you go to bed *that night,* give yourself a boring, fifteen-minute punishment for *each* check for that day. Here are a few sample punishments, to give you some ideas:

- Sweep and mop the kitchen floor.
- If your family has a dishwasher, do that night's supper dishes by hand.
- Wash out socks by hand.
- Call someone on the phone who bores you, and talk for fifteen minutes.
- Read the measurements and abbreviations sections of a cookbook.
- Watch a television show you hate, for fifteen minutes. That's not counting commercials, because they can use up to sixteen minutes of every prime-time hour.
- Eat something boring for supper, like plain lettuce or bread.
- Copy fifteen entries from a dictionary, including accent marks, alternate uses, etc.
- Clean your mother's jewelry.

6.

Journey Into Your Own Head

You're a much more effective person than you were when you began reading this book, and for that, you should congratulate yourself. You assert your Rights with Skills that help you reach your goals in dealing with people. The reason why this is happening is because, without realizing it, you've been increasing your *awareness.*

You've had to become *aware* of yourself, maybe for the first time—aware of what you really want in all of your relationships, how you handle yourself, what you're doing that's right or wrong, and what can be done to strengthen both you as a person and your relationships.

Awareness is a constant process, and simple to understand. We can't become more aware of our *actions* without also being more aware of our *feelings,* as you learned in the chapter on friendship. We can't take steps to change what happens to us unless we go to the trouble of *identifying our feelings* about it in very specific terms, so we'll know exactly what needs to be changed. We usually begin this process by using our *senses.*

Dr. Joseph Zinker, of the Gestalt Institute in Cleveland, Ohio, developed this chart to show how our senses push us to take action, and how we can use them to "fatten our awareness."

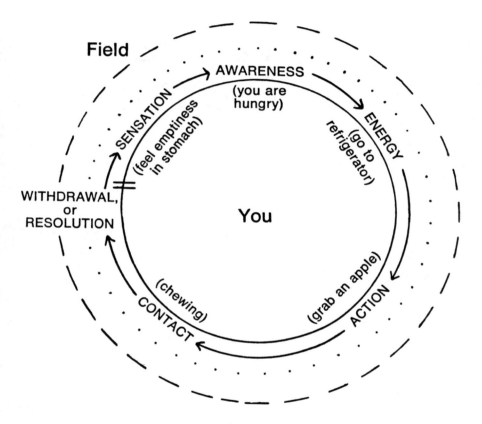

Begin reading the chart at "sensation," the point at which your senses tell you that something is wrong. In this example, the sensation is an emptiness in the stomach.

You identify that sensation and gain an *awareness* of the problem. This awareness can be "fat" or "thin"— either you are fully aware of what the problem is or you haven't asked enough questions to know exactly what is wrong yet. This example is simple; you are aware that the sensation (emptiness in the stomach) means that you are hungry.

Once you know that, some sort of initial energy is needed to begin solving the problem. You get up from your seat and go to the refrigerator, and go on to the action stage—you grab an apple.

The contact stage is crucial. Either you establish successful contact—chew up the apple and get rid of your hunger—or you spit it out and go hungry. Either way, you finish the contact and end up at withdrawal from the problem, or resolution of it. Your awareness of the problem is then over—unless, of course, you still sense an emptiness in your stomach, in which case the cycle begins again.

The large circle in the center, around which all of the senses and decisions revolve, is you. The larger circles around you are the "field," or everything that happens outside of you. Sometimes, according to Zinker, we are influenced by those outer circles in our lives. They cause us to feel or be aware of things. But, whether or not you get around to a resolution that *cuts you off* from the original, troubling sensation, as in the diagram, is up to *you*.

Zinker goes on to give three basic steps to "fattening" our awareness:

1. Ask questions, as many as it takes for you to know what the right energy and action steps will be.
2. Get feedback—answers for your questions, and reactions to the energy and action steps you choose. In other words, *before* you finish the contact and withdrawal stages, be evaluating your actions along the way. Remember Right No. 3: *You have the right to change your mind* if what you're doing isn't what will work best for you.
3. Acknowledge what you learn. Telling others—or talking to yourself—about what you discover, and new ways in which you feel your awareness "fattening," will make

you even more aware. And other people's reactions will add even more awareness from the "field" about your feelings and possible consequences.

You can apply this "fattening awareness" cycle to any problems in your relationships, by using all of the steps. This example will give you an idea of how it's done:

Sensation:	You feel ticked off at the maître d' in a busy restaurant at lunchtime.
Awareness:	You realize that three couples have been seated before you and your friend, just because they're older. You've been waiting the longest, and it's not fair.
Energy:	You think for a moment about what you're going to say, and announce to your friend that you're going to protest.
Action:	You walk up to the maitre d' and tell him that you've noticed that he's showing people to tables who just walked in, when it's been your turn for a long time. You add that if you're not seated immediately, you and your friend will spend your money elsewhere, and you'll inform your parents and friends of the lousy service here.
Contact:	You return to your place in line and watch the maître d' seat yet another couple who just arrived. You walk out and go to another restaurant.
Withdrawal or Resolution:	You follow through on your awareness of being discriminated against, by writing a letter of protest to the restaurant's manager, and telling your parents and friends how you were treated. You can also congratulate yourself for acting so assertively. You may not change the maitre d's be-

havior, but you took the right steps to correct an injustice toward you.

EXERCISE

Think of a problem in a current relationship. It can be a disagreement with an authority or equal relationship, or a recent hassle you had with someone in a commercial position.

Using the "fattening awareness" chart, write the steps you would like to take to solve the problem, in the spaces below. If you can't quite identify the root of the problem—and, therefore, can't come up with the right action to solve it—go over the steps for fattening awareness. Ask more questions: When is it that you sense the trouble most intensely? Are you with the other person when you feel troubled, or alone? What's happening at the time to make you feel upset? Why is it happening? Would talking to the other person—using your negotiation skills—be a contact step that would bring results that would satisfy you? Try to make yourself *aware* of the consequences of different actions you could take, and work out the solution that would seem, at this point, to work best for both of you.

Sensation: _____

Awareness: _____

Energy: _____

Action: _____

Contact: _____

Withdrawal or Resolution: _____

As you've done in other exercises that ironed out problems in relationships, go to the person with your plan. Part of your action or contact steps is likely to be an explanation that you've become aware of these bad vibes, and what you would like to do about it. If your plan doesn't work, or if the other person doesn't buy it, try an *alternative* solution.

PUTTING YOUR SENSES TO WORK

Senses aren't only for sniffing out trouble. They're grand tools for discovering things that aren't always obvious on the surface, and making use of them can increase your awareness of forces and dynamics you've never imagined. Awareness seems to be one of those neat things that's *cumulative*—it piles up on top of itself, feeding your next discoveries. The more you do it, the more it happens.

Here's an experiment that's fun, and it's not too difficult. For one week, observe things with all of your senses, instead of just seeing them. When you look at a dusty corner, imagine the smell of old dust. After a hard rain, stand outside and smell the wet pavement (you really can), and notice the shine on the leaves. As they touch against each other in the wind, listen to the soft sound; it's as though they give happy, little kisses. Look at a friend of the opposite sex and imagine feeling the texture and thickness of his or her hair. Close your eyes and feel your own. Notice the different degrees of sweetness one food has if it rests on different taste buds.

As you look and taste and touch, see things from as many different positions as you can. Think of what nature did to give something its feel or taste. Trust your senses for the week, and act as though the things your *senses* tell you, not what you have been taught, are reality. Know that those things are all yours. *Reach* with your senses, and have faith that they represent what is real.

At the end of the week, write a few paragraphs about what you "saw" or learned that you never noticed before. Write down how it felt to make yourself aware of how many things your senses can tell you. The sky's the limit with these paragraphs, and you can make them sound any way you like, without worrying that anyone will ever read them. You will use them as your very first entry in your *journal*, which will be one of the most special, private, and exciting things you will ever do for yourself.

KEEPING A JOURNAL

It's difficult sometimes to keep track of our feelings and sort them out. When you're trying to solve a long-term problem in a relationship, the process is a lot easier if you have a way of remembering how you felt about things a month ago.

A journal is the way. Journals aren't only good for sorting out problems, though; I use mine to let off steam in all kinds of moods—silly, bursting with joy, wallowing in self-pity, or so mad I can't see straight. I even write down my dreams sometimes.

What makes a journal so special is that it's your own, private *expression*. Anything goes in those pages—dirty pictures, hateful gossip, or your most intimate wants. We all have feelings we can't—or won't—share with anyone. By keeping a journal, you get to *express* those feelings anyway, without embarrassing or hurting anyone.

Everyone would be a little less tense if they would tune in to themselves through a journal. It's not meant to be shared, though—that's *your* place to find shelter.

Starting a journal is easy; all you have to do is pick it up and write. Some people use a spiral note pad. There are different types of bound, hard-cover "books" with blank pages available at most bookstores. They're not expensive —only one to three dollars—and they'll take a lot of wear and tear, and last forever. I always buy the same kind, and label them "Volume One," "Volume Two," and so on, as I fill them up.

TUNING IN TO YOURSELF

Learning about being in touch with our feelings and senses gives us a new perspective—a new way of looking at things. As we know more about the different *angles* of situations, we know more about the different *alternatives* open to us, and how to choose the one that will work best. And that, folks, is why awareness is so important—besides the fact that it just makes life a lot more interesting!

In chapter one, you took a quiz and wrote a theme—based on the answers you gave—that presented your *feelings* in dozens of areas. The sentences below (now that you've explored your feelings) will show you how those feelings cause you to *behave*. Each one is an open sentence, which you'll complete with a statement about the way you act. Examples:

1. When people ignore me, I *ask them why they're treating me that way.*
2. When I like something I just did, I *go and tell someone about it.*
3. When I'm feeling generous, I *buy food for my friends.*

There are several stages to this exercise. You'll be using your answers for the next part, so complete the sentences listed below before you go on.

_____ 1. When people ignore me, I _____

_____.

_____ 2. When I like something I just did, I _____

_____.

_____ 3. When I feel generous, I _____

_____.

_____ 4. When I receive praise, I _____

_____.

_____ 5. When someone likes me but I don't like him or her back, I _____.

_____ 6. When I know I've hurt someone's feelings, I _____.

_____ 7. I'm best around people when I _____ _____.

_____ 8. When I feel lonely, I _____ _____.

_____ 9. When I feel jealous, I_____ _____.

_____ 10. When someone gives me affection, I _____ _____.

_____ 11. I hurt others when I _____ _____.

_____ 12. I feel guilty when I _____ _____.

_____ 13. When I'm angry, I _____ _____.

_____ 14. When someone is angry at me, I _____ _____.

_____ 15. I could never tell anyone that I _____ _____.

_____ 16. I wish I could tell everyone that I _____ _____.

_____ 17. I don't like myself much when I _____ _____.

_____ 18. When someone puts me down, I _____ _____.

_____ 19. I get a real big boost when I _____

_____.

_____ 20. When I learn something about myself, I ____

_____.

_____ 21. When I like someone who doesn't like me
back, I _____.

_____ 22. When I feel awkward around others, I ____

_____.

_____ 23. When a friend lets me down, I _____

_____.

_____ 24. When I let down a friend, I _____

_____.

_____ 25. I run away from people after I _____

_____.

_____ 26. When I feel really lazy and something needs
to be done, I _____.

_____ 27. When friends try to control me, I _____

_____.

_____ 28. When I feel that I "belong" or am really "into"
a group of people, I _____

_____.

_____ 29. When I feel afraid of another person, I ____

_____.

_____ 30. When something confuses me, I _____

_____.

_____ 31. I get down on myself when I _____

_____.

_____ 32. I feel ashamed when I _____

_____.

_____ 33. I feel embarrassed after I _____

_____.

Did you surprise yourself with any of your answers? It's not often that we think about our behavior in such *specific* terms—most people, in fact, just aren't that *aware* of what they do.

The next step is to put an X in front of the behaviors on this list that you *don't like*. Don't worry about how many X's there are or feel bad if you have a lot. It only means that you're aware of that many ways in which you want to be a more effective person, and there's nothing wrong with that!

Now, the next step is to take each statement about your behavior that you X'd, and rewrite it in the form of a *resolution* (like a New Year's resolution). Here is an example:

Statement: When I like something I just did, I *go and tell someone about it.*

Resolution: When I like something I do from now on, I'm going to *give myself a treat.*

You can use this chart, or make a bigger one like it, to write down your resolutions and keep track of how well you stick to each one. Over the next three weeks, when you've stuck to a resolution, put a check mark in the space for that week. (Don't try to be Superman or Wonder Woman—if you've followed a resolution once for one week, mark it on the chart and forget about that one for the rest of the week. Go on to the other resolutions on your list!)

Resolutions	Week 1	Week 2	Week 3
1.			
2.			
3.			
4.			
5.			

The last stage of this exercise is the most fun—and the easiest to remember.

Every week, look at the new checks you made during that week. Each one, you know, represents something *you* did, on your own, to make yourself a better person in your own eyes. That calls for a reward.

So, for *each* new improvement for that week, give yourself a fifteen-minute reward. These rewards should be real treats, not things you ordinarily do anyway, and they should be things that will make you *happy* to do. Here are a few sample rewards I use for myself, to give you some ideas:

● Make a long-distance call to an old friend. (Be sure to clear it with your folks, and pay for the call yourself.)

● Spend fifteen minutes alone, listening to a favorite album and daydreaming.

● Make tacos for yourself and a few friends.

● Pamper your body with a facial or hair treatment, a massage, or a manicure.

● Buy some fresh flowers for your room.

● Do Jacobsen's relaxation exercise.

COOL AS A CUCUMBER?

This is another experiment that will make you more aware of yourself—and help you to change what you don't like.

First, sit down with a dictionary and copy *any* fifty adjectives. (In case you usually take your afternoon nap during English class, an adjective is a word that *describes* something: blue, large, gentle, brave, nasty.)

Look at the list when you've finished. How many adjectives do you *wish* applied to you, but they don't? Copy those on a new list.

Beside each word on the new list—words that you would like to apply to you—write a phrase giving a *symbol,* or *metaphor,* of that word. Below are examples of what I mean:

gentle: *Gentle* as a baby lamb.
strong: *Strong* as a gladiator.
eager: *Eager* as a kid on the last day of school.

As you write each phrase, think of the one thing that best *symbolizes* each word for you, and use it. Make the symbols something or someone *you* would like to be compared to.

When your list is finished, hang it on your dresser mirror, where you can't miss it when you get up in the morning. If you read your list every day while you're getting dressed—especially if you listen to some favorite music at the same time—it will inspire you a little; you'll feel more like going out and *being* like that as you start your day.

You can add new adjectives and symbols to your list anytime, and erase old ones as you feel they come to describe you.

There are variations to this exercise that are fun to do with friends. You can take your original list of fifty adjectives and mark those which *already* apply to you. Then, show the list to a friend, ask him or her to mark those which describe you, and see how differently other people see you! Your friend can make a separate list of fifty adjectives for himself (or herself), and the two of you can go through the same process with your friend's list.

SHOW YOUR COLORS!

The lists from the above exercise, plus the theme you wrote in chapter one "Everything That Matters about [your name]"), will come in handy for this project.

Flags are made of symbols—why not make a flag that symbolizes *you*? It shouldn't be too hard now to figure out specifically which symbols might represent you—you've done more thinking about yourself and what makes you tick, through the exercises in this book, then many people do in their lifetime!

The flag of the United States, for instance, contains stars and stripes as symbols of the states. Your flag, too, can represent anything about you. You can use colors that express things you feel. If you're a nature lover, you can make your symbols from natural materials—oak leaves to make a tree if you think you're "strong like a mighty oak," or walnut shells if you're a "tough nut to crack." The size, texture, and design of your flag can end up being anything that will represent you and your values.

Hang it in your room, and when you look at your flag, you'll be reminded of what you are. Or, as your values change, you might be reminded of what you *aren't* anymore, and you'll want to change your flag to reflect changes you make in yourself! ˙

VALUES TO BURN

Set a timer for two minutes. While the timer is counting away the seconds, pretend that your house is burning down around you. Everything will be destroyed, but you have two minutes to choose any *ten* things you could rescue from the fire. What would they be? Write down the ten possessions you would save. Don't go over ten, and if you haven't thought of that many by the time your two minutes are up, stop writing anyway—the house is gone.

Look at your list. Why did you want to save those ten items over everything else in the house? What makes them so important or so special to you? Were your choices based on how expensive those things are, or how unique? Or did you save things with sentimental value—special gifts from special friends, old family heirlooms, or something you had made yourself? If you spend a minute thinking about each one, you'll learn a lot about your *values*—how you decide what's important to you.

This would be a good game to play with your family, especially during the Powwow discussions you began back in chapter three. Since the members of your family are all familiar with basically the same items as you are, it would be fun to make your lists together, then compare them. Each person should be given a chance to explain why he or she would save certain items. You'll learn a lot about what's important to others in your family—money, good artwork, preserving the family's heritage, reminders of loved ones, or a mixture of those things. You might even find that others would save some of the same things as you—but for totally different reasons!

"THIS IS MY BOX!"

In the first opera written for television, "Amahl and the Night Visitors" by Gian Carlo Menotti, Kaspar the Wise Man carried a special box. Kaspar's box had three drawers in it. A favorite scene in that Christmas show had Kaspar revealing the secret contents of his box to wide-eyed Amahl, a little crippled boy.

In the first drawer of his box, Kaspar stored "magic

7.

School, Jobs, and Other Pressure Pains

In the same way that we can have the *most* control over relationships in which we are "equal" (if we *use* our control, that is)—friends, schoolmates, brothers and sisters—we have the *least* control over *authority* relationships.

There's no getting around it. Parents, teachers, and people for whom we work, all have power over us. They control our grades, what kind of wages we make, and how much freedom we have. If we don't have any cash (from authority), we're cut off from doing a lot of things we'd like to do. If we don't make decent grades, our parents might chop away even more freedom. Or, we might be stopped from pursuing other interests in school—athletic teams, class or club offices, taking certain courses—if we don't meet someone's (an authority's) standards. Authority affects our lives in a big way.

Our parents don't let us see the pressures they're under, so it's natural for us to figure that, as we get older, the pressure stops. That's not how it works, though—if your parents have "made it," it means they probably spent thousands of hours doing work they were sick to death of, after they spent hundreds of hours in classes they hated as much as you hate yours. And all along the way, in order to keep making it, they probably had to play up to their bosses, and didn't like doing it.

We have more options—more choices open to us. But that, too, is a pressure. We have to make more decisions than our folks made, sometimes we're pressed to make them at a younger age, and the decisions are harder to make because we have so much more from which to choose.

Enough of this depressing forecast—the point is that, in some way, there's always someone to answer to. Now, how do we cope?

It's true that if we don't act in ways that please those in positions of authority over us, they can use some of that authority to come down on us.

But, it is our *fear* of that happening—not the *likelihood* that it will—that keeps us from being assertive when we deal with authority!

We have less power in authority relationships, but that *doesn't* mean we have no rights, or that we shouldn't use our assertiveness Skills to stand up for those rights. We do have less control over the *outcome,* or results, of situations involving teachers, parents, and bosses. But, doesn't that seem like *more* of a reason to put our assertiveness Skills to work?

Authority shouldn't intimidate, or scare, us. We do have to realize that final decisions about things affecting us—grades, working hours, pay, freedom-to-move-around issues—may be up to someone else. That's our tough luck. But, realizing that, it makes sense to go ahead and use our assertiveness Skills at their *best* when we deal with authority, and do everything we can to make sure that those decisions are in our favor. When we think decisions by authorities are unfair—or we feel as though pressure from an authority is unreasonable—there are ways to appeal, or complain about, the situation. You'll learn how that's done in a later chapter.

One important thing to remember, though, is *not* to go against authority *just* to see if you can do it. That's not being assertive, it's being cocky, and you're likely to end up with *no* power in the situation at all. Assertiveness should be used with authority on the same basis as you use it with friends—when the situation calls for it.

EXERCISE

In this exercise, you are given a number of specific tasks to perform in dealing with authority figures. You can choose anyone in a position of authority over you for each task—teachers, counselors, parents, employers, coaches, or any other person who "supervises" you in any way.

There is no time limit on this exercise because you can't create all of the situations in which you will do these things—you may have to wait until the opportunity presents itself. Try to finish within a couple of weeks, though, so the situations will be fresh in your mind.

The intent of the exercise is to practice using the Skills you've learned, with people who have the final say about some part of your life, or can put pressure on you in some way. After the list of tasks, you'll find a chart you can use to keep track of how assertively you behaved in each instance, just as you've done in past exercises.

1. Give a sincere compliment to a teacher or some other professional person in your life, regarding some aspect cf his or her *work* that impressed you.
2. Question a doctor, dentist, or counselor about a prescription, medication, or other aspect of treatment he or she has chosen for you. Be concerned and sincerely curious with your questions, and be persistent. Don't stop until you understand the explanation completely, even if it takes a long time.

3. Ask a teacher (or other person speaking to a group you are in) to further explain something you don't understand, even if you think you're the only person in the group who isn't catching on.
4. Complain to a doctor, dentist, lawyer, or other professional person that what he or she is doing—or has just done—is not, you feel, in your best interest, or could have been handled in a better way. Allow him or her time to explain why things were done in that manner. If no explanation is offered, or you feel that your opinion wasn't taken seriously, take a look at chapter ten to find out what you can do about it.
5. Ask a favor—not a large one, but important to you— from someone in a position of authority over you. Be prepared with good reasons for your request and a way to pay it back. Choose one listed below, or come up with one of your own.

● Ask your boss, if you have a job, for some time off. (Offer to make it up at another time.)

● Ask your boss for a raise—*if* you think you deserve it.

● Ask a teacher to look at something you did on your own time.

● Ask your parents to allow you to go someplace you've never been before, at least not on your own.

How did it go? Were you able to use assertive body language to help get your point across? As you've done with previous exercises like this one, fill in your chart and *evaluate* your experience. If you're still weak in some areas, review the sections on body assertiveness (page 77). If you feel it will help you, go back and redo one or two exercises in that section, too, to strengthen your Skills during a confrontation.

	Person	Situa-tion	What Satisfied Me about How I Acted	What I Didn't Like about My Behavior	My Over-all Feel-ing about the Contact —Good, Bad
1. Compliment					
2. Question Treatment					
3. Explain					
4. Complain					
5. Favor					

I'M NOT HASSLED, I'M JUST BUSY

Stress, pressure, tension, being hassled—they're all ways of saying we live with *anxiety*. By training yourself to behave assertively, you're learning a lot about how to deal with situations that cause anxiety. The point you want to reach is where the *sudden impact* of a stress-producing situation—the time when you're numb, shocked, panicky —is over almost immediately, and you're able to carry on rationally until things settle down.

Some people live in a continual state of panic. One of the easiest ways to be that way is always to feel that things are closing in on you—too much homework to do, too many chores, not enough money, clothes don't look right, nothing works. The mistake that's easy to make— that gets us to that panicky, closed-in feeling—is spending *time* thinking and moaning about it, instead of taking steps to deal with our problems.

There are times when being a little bit depressed can work *for* us, as we'll learn in chapter nine. What we're talking about here is living *inside* our depression most of the time, and not reaching a "healing" point right after a crisis.

When you feel pressure most of the time, and think there's no way out, you're reaching to things *outside* of you, and ignoring everything *inside* that could get you out. Pressure doesn't have to come from authority or a life-or-death situation to ruin your day, either. A put-down from a friend you respect, or a minor encounter with a stranger, can upset you and qualify as a crisis. In fact, *anything* qualifies as a "crisis" if it keeps you from concentrating on what you want to do, brings you down, and makes small pressures seem bigger than they actually are. And when you think about it, isn't the main point in learning to be effective, to make sure that doesn't happen anymore—to become skillful in dealing with people, so that *you* determine how you'll feel and act every day?

GETTING THEM OFF YOUR BACK

The pressure situations in this quiz are more *subtle* (sly, not so obvious) than crises like getting suspended from school or getting arrested. But it is the more subtle kind of pressure that brings us down and builds up to a *real* problem. The subtle pressures in life keep the tranquilizer companies going.

Take the quiz, circle your answer to each question, then read on to see if your assertiveness Skills are ready for pressure encounters of the irritating kind.

1. It's been a bad day all around—you got up late, your hair is filthy, and your mother just asked you to walk

three blocks to the store—in a cold rain—for one lousy quart of milk. In the store, a member of a religious cult, which has had a lot of bad publicity, tries to sell you a box of candy. You told him three times that you weren't interested, but he won't go away, and you're fed up. You:

a. Walk over to the store manager's office and ask to speak with someone about being pestered by solicitors on the store's property.
b. Buy a box of candy so the guy will shut up and leave you alone.
c. Let him follow you and go on with his pitch—you already told him you're not going to buy any candy, so if he wants to waste his time and energy, that's his problem.
d. Get into a discussion about his cult, figuring that maybe if you're nice to him, he'll go away more easily.

2. All of your friends are into running, and so are you. They've all spent a lot of money on running outfits and are pressuring you to do the same. But you're really serious about building up your endurance and distance, and you know that to do that, you've got to get a pair of good running shoes. Still, your friends look pretty sharp when they go trotting around the neighborhood in their fancy duds, and you feel a little left out. You have the money for either the shoes or the outfit, but not both. You:

a. Go ahead and buy the outfit. It's better to fit in, and your sneakers should hold up for a few more months.
b. Instead of pouting around your friends, tell them what's on your mind. Be honest about feeling a little left out, even if it means you'll get teased for being too serious. Then, buy the shoes you know you need for endurance running.
c. Tell your friends how ridiculous they look when they

parade around in their splashy outfits, how you think they got ripped off when they bought them, and that you wouldn't be caught dead in those costumes.

d. Ask one of your friends to go with you to buy some running shoes. Who knows, maybe you'll find a really cheap pair and have enough dough for an outfit, too.

3. Your history class was divided into groups of eight students each, for a special project. You were selected as leader of your group. Your job is to assign certain tasks to each person in the group, then the group will make an oral presentation to the class a week from now. You're trying to be fair, but some of the kids won't cooperate, and no one wants to do the less interesting tasks. Suddenly, this business of telling others what to do leaves a bad taste in your mouth—you don't feel like a good leader, and you're afraid your group will get a bad grade because of it. You:

a. Go to the teacher and complain that the other kids won't cooperate with you. Tell her you're not going to let this class make a fool of you.

b. Face it, you can't handle leadership. Turn the job over to someone who will do it right.

c. Let things go on as they are, and trust that as the one-week deadline gets closer, the group will pull *itself* together.

d. Level with the other kids in the group. Tell them you're not having the easiest time as leader, and you'd appreciate it if they would stop bickering and pitch in. Ask for suggestions on how they'd like to get the job done. Tell them you're also considering asking the teacher for advice on organizing a group; see what they think of that idea.

4. You're eating lunch in the school cafeteria, and you overhear people at the next table slamming your friend Carla. They're really putting her down, and you're not going to listen to it anymore. You:

a. Turn around and calmly tell them that if they're going to talk about someone they should be more quiet about it, because her friends might hear them.
b. Ignore the clods.
c. Announce that you're Carla's best friend, and they'd better stop talking about her—or else!
d. Tell Carla what you heard, and who said it. If people are going to say such nasty things about her, she has a right to know!

5. Mr. Castovich, a teacher, was just fired from your school. Most of the students, including you, like the guy a lot. About a hundred students are organizing a "Save Mr. Castovich" campaign. The plans include petitions to be signed by both students and parents, and a student strike if he's not rehired, and you're wanted to help lead the effort. The problem is, even though you like Mr. Castovich, you think the reason he got canned was a good one, and he shouldn't get his job back. Still, you don't want to look like a traitor or hurt Mr. Castovich's feelings. You:
a. Go with the campaign. It'll be a real victory for the students if Castovich gets his job back, whether he deserves it or not.
b. Refuse to work with the campaign and make your support of the firing known to everyone. Maybe, instead of a traitor, you'll come out of it looking like a hero.
c. Try to talk your friends out of starting the campaign. If they can be persuaded to drop the whole idea, the pressure will be off of you to take a stand.
d. Quietly refrain from supporting the campaign. In the meantime, send a letter to Mr. Castovich, explaining that you like and respect him as a person, but you must follow your beliefs, as he did. Don't apologize for your position, but do wish him luck.

Answers

1. The answer that works best is (a). After you politely ask someone to leave you alone several times, the best action is to let the store manager know you're being bothered. Most places of business don't allow solicitors —salespeople, political workers, or anyone "peddling" any kind of merchandise or ideas—on their premises. They know that if shopping in their store becomes a pain in the neck, people won't shop there anymore. They'll appreciate your telling them about it, so don't be afraid to complain.

    The other answers—buying the candy, letting the guy go on with his pitch, or discussing his work—will only make the situation worse. He'll never leave.

2. If you answered (a), you're giving in to someone else's values, though you disagree with them. The last answer, (d), is a little more workable, but you're still *being manipulated* away from your own goal—a good pair of running shoes. This is on top of the fact that if you *are* serious about running, even a couple of miles at a time, good shoes will be your number-one priority. Otherwise, you can expect to join thousands of weekend joggers who thought they'd save some money and ended up with a busted sciatic nerve (including me). It hurts —for years—and the best way to get it is to run in sneakers.

    Insulting your friends, (c), won't get you anywhere. When you put them down, you just put distance between them and you—when what you're worried about is getting closer to them! If you chose (b), you trust your values enough to say, "This is me. I don't mind what you're into, even though it's different from the things I like." You can still be friends and have fun together, without feeling *pressured* to be just like them.

3. The first three choices, if you look at them closely, are

all cop-outs. You accepted a responsibility, and now is not the time to crumble under a little pressure.

The other students would have given the leader a hard time, no matter who it was. So you have to resist the temptation to take this type of pressure too personally. The best answer is (d). It's much more assertive to be honest about your fears than to run away from them. With this answer, you're giving a little more authority to others in your group, but still guiding the whole thing. Your title, remember, is "leader," not "commander."

4. Choosing (a) will let the gossipers know they're being obnoxious without getting *you* into trouble. Ignoring the conversation would be too much to expect; it's awfully hard to ignore something that's upsetting you. Answer (c) sounds like a challenge to a fight—and could end up that way. The last answer is cruel. You're not doing your friend a favor if you tell her the bad things people say about her, you're just hurting her feelings. Honest, constructive criticism from *you* is fine, to her face. But if you have something to say to your friend, do it without telling her that people are talking behind her back.

5. The first answer is spineless, the second is selfish, and the third is just plain phony. In all three, you're thinking only of yourself, and what other people might think or say about you. You aren't showing much respect for your fellow students, who probably are very sincere in their fight to save Castovich's job. You also aren't considering Mr. Castovich's feelings. Most importantly, you're not being true to your own beliefs. The last answer is the best one—you're doing what you think is right (and what will make you like and respect *yourself*), without interfering with anyone else's rights. The letter to Mr. Castovich isn't absolutely necessary, but its a kind gesture that will show him you're trying to do the right thing. It's always OK to explain your behavior

if you do it to *clarify* your reasons, and not to *apologize* for them.

How did your assertiveness Skills hold up under subtle pressure? If you answered three or more of the questions correctly, they held up pretty well.

If you missed more than two, part of the problem might be that you don't always know where your pressure is coming from, let alone what you can do about it. Often, we know we're uncomfortable or full of anxiety, but don't figure out what made us feel that way until hours, or even days, later. If this happens to you a lot, go back to chapter six and review the section on "fattening your awareness." Then, when you feel *really* aware of the dynamics happening around you, read these questions again. You'll understand a little better what subtle pressure is, and which of your assertiveness Skills you'll need in coping with it.

DECISIONS, DECISIONS

One of the hairiest kinds of subtle pressure is having to make decisions. This is especially true if you've never made a particular decision before and aren't too sure about the consequences of *any* of your choices.

Some of our decisions affect us for only a day or two—what to wear today, what to get Dad for his birthday, how hard do I need to study for that Spanish test, and so on. These short-term decisions are enough of a hassle. But when we get into more serious, long-term decisions, our days can get pretty rough: Should I go to college? How do I know if the work I choose will really mean anything to me? Should I continue this relationship? Should I have sex?

Decision-making *can* be boiled down to a simple process: Be aware of the alternatives, weigh them, choose one that looks as if it will work best, and follow through with it. If it doesn't work, start over with another alternative.

Sounds simple, doesn't it?

Well, it's not. It *would* be if we could also know the consequences of each action we might take, before we act. Unfortunately, we can't always know that. And if it's a serious decision we're making, such as what to study in college, we end up enduring a lot of baloney—and maybe wasting a lot of time—in the process of correcting our mistakes.

There *is* a way for decision-making to become less painful. Whenever you make a decision, you're actually taking a small step to make your life a little better, a little more satisfying, than the life you've known so far. *This is your goal,* every day. When you're confused and trying to make long-term decisions about your future—and the years leading to adulthood are unfairly crammed with decisions like that—a question like "Should I go to college?" can drive a person batty.

When all you draw is blanks, which is what can happen when a big decision has to be made, it's time to forget the question. That's right, forget it—and ask other questions instead. Let's use the "college or not" dilemma as an example.

"Should I go to college?" is a ridiculous question. It has no meaning and no answer makes sense, because you've never been there. It's too big, too unknown, and too scary to deal with. There are, though, a lot of other questions that *do* make sense:

- What have I expected from education in the past?
- Did I get what I expected? If not, was it education's fault or mine?
- What can I do, or what can I learn to do?
- What have I never tried that would make me happy to learn something about? Could I handle doing it every

day? Would I work hard enough at learning it to become good at it?

- What would I do with a year off after high school? How would I live? What could I do during that year to get closer to a decision about my future?
- What can I afford? Where does my family fit in?

The list could go on for pages. These are all questions you *can* answer, because you have knowledge and experience to draw from. By seriously asking questions of this sort, you'll provide yourself with the answer to the bigger, scarier question. Your answers—and the knowledge of yourself you've gained from doing the exercises in this book—will tell you if college will help you to reach your goals or if another route makes more sense.

In making any big decision, while you're asking the questions and weighing your alternatives, these three points can keep the problem in focus. Remember them; tape them to your mirror if it will help:

1. The *meaning* of a decision—why you make the choices you do—is every bit as important as what you end up doing.
2. Part of the outcome of any decision should be that you will *like and respect yourself* afterward. Do what must be done to accomplish that, and accept the consequences.
3. Mistakes are only detours. They can be corrected.

YOUR NAME IN LIGHTS?

Making decisions doesn't always have to be a chore. This experiment, for instance, can help you sort out some questions about your future and have a laugh, too.

Imagine yourself ten years from now—what you're doing, where you live, who lives with you—and write a newspaper about it. This is a good project to do with friends, and read your "newspapers" aloud to each other when you're finished.

The name of the paper is "The   (your name)
Times," and you'll want to include these columns and features:

Front-Page News	Entertainment
Lost and Found	Cartoons
For Sale	Police Report
Wanted to Buy	Vital Statistics
Sports	Local (family, close friends) News
Editorials	Society Column
Travel News	Business Report
"Dear Abby"	

You might surprise yourself and uncover a few new fears, dreams, or skills you hadn't taken seriously before. How does your present life fit into your ten-year forecast? This project should stimulate some thinking about how close you are to the kind of life you'd like to lead, and what sorts of changes will have to be made in the next few years. If you're in high school and trying to make decisions about your future, it would be a good idea to show your "newspaper" to a guidance counselor. He or she will be able to tell you what steps you need to plan on taking, in order to shape the kind of life you outlined as a "reporter" here.

8.

Alone— Maybe, But Not Lonely!

We've covered a lot of ground in regard to being effective with others—now, how effective are you with *yourself?* Are you comfortable in your own company? Can you enjoy spending two or three evenings—in a row—alone, without going crazy from boredom?

It's important to be able to answer yes to those questions, because if you can't offer *yourself* worthwhile and enjoyable companionship, how can you offer that to other people? An assertive person can enjoy both solitude *and* being with friends.

Many people can't stand to be alone; they're afraid to. Instead, they end up wasting an enormous amount of time with people they don't really like, just to avoid being by themselves. This kind of insecurity is dangerous—it puts severe limits on what you can do or what you can be. It often leads to getting married just to be "rescued," and that sort of partnership can be a bummer.

The ability to be *alone* effectively is—like asserting yourself with others—a Skill that has to be practiced. All of us are alone sometimes, so it's obviously better to be able to use and *enjoy* those hours than to have to suffer through them. When you're alone, you develop your own thoughts and opinions. If you can do that, you'll have a lot more to offer in relationships with others, because you won't *depend* on them so much. You'll be able to give something worthwhile, from a position of strength, rather than do all of the taking.

In this chapter, you're going to practice being alone *well*, especially when you're feeling down. We'll talk about doing things alone and meeting people on your own. Since so many of us aren't used to being by ourselves, though, let's start with something *easy*.

PLEASURE YOURSELF

Plan to spend one night this week completely *alone*. Since you've told your parents all about your work to become an effective person, and shown them this book, it shouldn't be too hard to get their cooperation.

This evening is all yours, and you should spend the whole time pampering yourself. Take a two-hour bath by candlelight. Do some reading you've been putting off, eat chocolate, write a poem. Bask in self-love for the evening. You'll get the most out of this experiment if you plan what you'll do ahead of time, and *don't* work too hard at enjoying yourself. Don't plan on more than two or three different things to do; the idea is to get maximum pleasure from pampering yourself and from spending the evening alone. If you schedule too many things to do that night, you'll feel obligated to a timetable and forget to relax and enjoy yourself.

The next day, write a page or two in your journal about the experience. Did it get boring after a while? Did you feel a little guilty, lavishing all that love on yourself? (Don't feel badly if you did; it's normal.) Or did you relax and think about the things you usually don't take the time to think out? Overall, how good are you at being alone? Maybe you came up with a nice fantasy or daydream—write it down if you did; it will be nice to escape with someday.

DEPRESSION—NOT A DEATH SENTENCE

It would be silly to try to convince readers that getting depressed is fun; we all know it's not. But it *can* be awfully interesting.

We can put depression to use, by not getting lost in it. The key is to be an *outside* observer to your own bad mood. Sit back and look at it, as though it were happening to someone else.

Don't fight depression when you feel it coming on. It will *go away faster*—and without that lingering sadness that keeps you from doing things you enjoy—if you follow this strategy:

Accept it. When we try to escape a depressing time with food or booze, we accomplish nothing, and create more problems. It's just as bad to surround yourself with a crowd, especially if you're not really into being with those people. Doing those things will only make you sadder.

Let the sadness come. *Watch* it come. Quiet your mind, light a candle, be alone, and use your senses. What made you sad? Does the same thing always make you sad? Why does it happen—what could you do to change things so that the situation won't always get you down? How about your Rights—have you been asserting them? As you look at your depression and ask questions, *let the sadness keep coming.* You've heard of the "river of sadness"? Well, a river won't dry up until it runs its *natural* course. Sadness is natural—let it sweep over you naturally, being *aware* the whole time of what is happing to you. You're not trying to keep it away, but you *are* staying on top of it.

Accept the fact that everybody gets bummed out. Tell yourself, "Well, now it's my turn. Let's get started and see what happens."

Use it. As the depression comes, remind yourself that you've set aside this chunk of time as a learning-and-growing session. Rather than feeling down and dull, you'll find yourself feeling a little more alive, aware, and nourished by the experience. Your best discovery, though, will be that your depression will be over much more quickly than it used to, and you won't carry it around with you for days!

GO ON YOUR OWN

Leaving the house alone can be a pretty scary thing to do, because you don't have friends with you to lean on. But, if you're interested in meeting new people—and most of us are—you can't do it with half a dozen giggling friends watching every move you make!

Going places by yourself is another of those "fear-of-the-unknown" situations, and the only way to conquer that fear is to turn it into a sense of adventure!

Several exercises follow, which will help you get past that fear and accept the challenge of being with people you don't know. As you do the exercises, remember these pointers:

Get rid of as many "unknowns" as you can. If you know ahead of time just *what* you'll be doing, it will be easy to concentrate on *that,* and have a good time. As a first step, put a check mark (√) in front of the categories on this list that interest you.

_____   Visiting friends or elderly relatives at home. ____

_____ Informal get-togethers. _____

_____ Church or school social activities. _____

_____ Crafts. _____

_____ Singing or playing musical instruments. _____

_____

_____ Biking, jogging, camping, or hiking. _____

_____

_____ Team sports. _____

_____ Learning foreign languages. _____

_____ Chess or checkers. _____

_____ Volunteer or political work. _____

_____

_____ Your town's history or architecture. _____

_____

_____ Other areas that interest you. _____

_____

Each of the above interests has the potential of leading to dozens of specific activities. After each category you checked off, using the space provided, write at least one *specific* activity you could participate in. For instance:

√   Crafts.   I could sign up for a class in stained glass.

√   Volunteer or political work. I could volunteer one day a week in a nursing home.

You've probably guessed the next step—choose one of the activities you selected, and do it. You should be able to find a club or organization in your city that sponsors activities, tournaments, or special events in all of the categories listed here. Or skim through the addresses in chapter ten for information on some national clubs.

Make this a project you will do alone, don't invite any friends to go along with you, because:

People you want to meet will be there. Everyone around you will be there for the same reason—taking part in an activity they enjoy. Some will be better at it than you, and many won't do as well. You'll show up with a built-in topic for conversation, though—what you're all doing—and the possibilities for meeting and talking with new people will be unlimited!

Once you take this step away from your small circle of friends, and begin rubbing elbows with some new people who share a mutual interest, you'll want to keep track of your behavior. Use this chart, and evaluate your performance for three weeks (or three meetings or activities):

	Week 1	Week 2	Week 3
How was my "body language"?			
Did I talk to anyone?			
Who? What did I say?			
How did people react to me?			
Did I judge my own performance, or did I compare myself to others?			
Which Rights did I forget to assert?			
Which Skills did I *not* use that would have helped?			
What can I do next time to improve?			
Did I use the Dropping-Clues Skill?			
Did I have a good time?			
Do I want to go back again?			

Evaluate your behavior for the first week—are you satisfied with the things you said and did? Actually, the only thing different about this experiment, for you, is the *setting*. You should be acting the way you normally do around friends. If you had a bad case of butterflies in your stomach the first time around, you're not concentrating enough on *what* you'll be doing. Make *that* your focus the next time, and you'll interact with the people more naturally.

STRANGERS CAN BE NICE PEOPLE

The exercise you just finished—joining a club that interests you—was included for the purpose of *expanding* your circle of friends and activities. It's a little different, though, to be around complete strangers when there is no common bond to tie you to them, such as a sport or a political cause. If you're still a little jittery about being alone in a group of strangers, this exercise wil give you a chance to practice.

The tasks on this first list are relatively easy because you don't have to say much to anyone. From these eleven specific tasks, choose *five* and do them:

1. Stand in a line—for a grocery check-out, movie tickets, or any other kind of waiting line—and say a sentence or two *about the line* to the person behind you. (If you choose this task, do it during the day.)
2. Carry a controversial book, with the title away from you, in public (*not* in school) for two hours.
3. Say "hi"—no more—to five strangers today. This one is easy in a crowded public place, such as a shopping mall.
4. Talk with the gas station attendant as he or she fills your tank.
5. Go to a bookstore in the evening, and browse for fifteen minutes. It's not necessary to speak to anyone.

6. Do a load of laundry in a laundromat you've never been to before.
7. Go to a free, outdoor concert alone. Stay until the concert is over.
8. Attend an art show alone.
9. Go on a group biking, hiking, or jogging excursion. You can invite a friend to go with you—but if you do, *you* arrive at the starting place twenty minutes earlier than your friend.
10. Attend a public hearing of a political issue in your town. (You'll find them listed in the newspaper.)
11. Someplace in which you're uninformed—for example, in an antique store—ask another customer for advice or information.

Well, how was it? Were you nervous? Since these tasks were relatively easy and involved little confrontation, it's not necessary to record your performance on a chart. Do write your feelings about the experience in your journal, however—which situations and places made you feel more comfortable than others, how people reacted to your friendly greetings, how you felt about your behavior in general.

Before you go on to the next list—which is a little more difficult—reward yourself! Buy an expensive magazine or a new album, or indulge in a hot fudge sundae. If you completed five of the tasks, you just grabbed a bit of independence for yourself. For that, you owe yourself a treat!

TALKING *WITH* PEOPLE, NOT *TO* THEM

Now you're ready for the "big time"—talking with people you don't know. You learned a little about initiating conversations in chapter two ("Dropping and Picking Up

Clues," page 43). This next exercise lets you practice doing just that—starting conversations.

To help you start your conversations, here are some more tips for talking with people you don't know. Feel free to copy these pointers and carry them with you if it will help to refresh your memory before you talk. (If you need to look at them, duck into a restroom or something—it won't be much of a "natural" conversation if you're reading questions from a piece of paper!)

Ways to Start a Conversation

- Ask a question or comment on something you're *both* doing. (Example: At an outdoor concert, "I think it's great that the musicians' union gives these free concerts, don't you?")
- Compliment someone on a skill. (Example: At a craft show, compliment an artist's work.)
- Ask a question, or make an observation, about what someone is doing. (Easy example: "Why are you doing that?")
- Ask someone if you can join him or her. (Example: In a park, "Mind if I share your bench?")
- Ask for advice, information, or an opinion. (Example: "Am I putting this bicycle chain on the right way?")
- Share an opinion or related experience. (Example: "I tried to make one of those once. I thought it would make a nice gift.")
- Greet a person and introduce yourself.

Additional Hints

- If you ask a question, be sure to wait for an answer.
- Don't let your questions—or information you offer about yourself—be too personal.
- Don't put yourself down, or start by saying, "I know this sounds stupid, but . . ."

- Don't make assumptions, or act as though you know something about the other person, or his or her work, that you really don't know.
- Ask "open-ended" questions—that is, questions that require more than a yes or no answer. It's not hard. Just word your questions so they begin with "what," "how," "who," "why," or "where."
- Remember your assertive body language and your right to say, "I don't know," or "I don't understand."

Remember that getting snubbed isn't the end of the world!

GO FORTH AND SPEAK!

As you did before, choose five tasks from this new list. As you complete each one, record what happens on the chart that follows—these encounters are more complicated than the first batch and involve the use of more of your assertiveness Skills, so you'll want to evaluate your performance when you're finished.

1. Introduce yourself to someone in a park, the library, or a class you're taking. Talk with the person for five minutes. If you can't keep the conversation going that long, try again with someone else. (Tasks on this list with time limits, like this one, don't count as "completed" unless you reach the time required.)
2. Conduct an opinion survey; you can use the results later in an article for your school paper or for a class assignment. Ask people's opinions on any issue you'd like. Do your interviewing in a public place—don't go door-to-door—and always introduce yourself first. State the purpose of your questioning, ask for a few moments of the person's time, and assure people that their name won't be used. (You needn't even ask their name.)

Question at least twenty people, one or two questions apiece.

3. Go to a coffee house in the evening. Don't go alone, but do ask your friends to stay on the other side of the room for a little while, so you can try out your experiment. Smile and nod at the first three people who look at you. Stay in the place for at least one hour. During that time, talk to someone you don't know for at least ten minutes.

4. Go jogging, swimming, or hiking alone. Have five-minute conversations with two different people during the afternoon. (It's perfectly all right, in these conversations, to tell people *why* you're talking with them. It might make the whole thing easier, and you'll already have something to talk about.)

5. Invite an elderly person walking in the same direction to walk with you. Introduce yourself, and offer to help carry something if he or she is loaded down.

6. Go to a folk dancing or square dancing class or social event, sponsored by a school, church, or your local "Y." Participate in the dancing. (NOTE: Summers are jammed with ethnic picnics and polka festivals on weekends. Check your newspaper. Either of these would qualify, and believe it or not, you'll have the time of your life!)

7. In a crowded restaurant, ask someone if you may share his or her table. Do it during the day, and choose someone of your own sex. It's not necessary to start a conversation for this one.

8. During intermission at a movie or concert, start a conversation with someone standing in the lobby. Choose someone of your own sex. (IMPORTANT: *Don't* invite trouble—have a friend waiting back at your seat for you. If you went to the show alone, *don't* do this task.)

9. Sit at the counter in a diner or luncheonette, and start a conversation with the person sitting next to you. Do this one during the day, but not at lunchtime—for

many working people, "lunch hour" is their only chance all day to get a little solitude and sort out their thoughts. Go at breakfast time or a little later in the afternoon.

	No. 1	No. 2	No. 3	No. 4	No. 5
With whom did I talk?					
What did I do, and where?					
What did I say?					
How did he or she react to me?					
Did I assert my Rights?					
Did I use the right Skills?					
What can I do next time to improve?					
How was my "body language"?					
How was my overall performance?					

First, if you completed five of the tasks, give yourself another reward—no matter how badly you think you did. Better yet, take two rewards. You've been pretty bold.

Now, how does your chart say you made out? The tasks should have been a little easier after you got through the first one or two. Which Rights didn't you assert—or, which Skills did you forget to use? How about that all-important body expression—calmness, loudness, posture?

If you think you did *very* poorly, don't be too upset. There's a good chance you did better than you thought, and it was the *other* person who was scared, or in too big a hurry to chat, or just plain unfriendly. Since you're not responsible for other people's behavior, don't worry about that. Just answer the questions on the chart honestly about *your* behavior, and practice some more to beef up your weak spots. If you feel you would do better with another go at it, repeat a task you particularly enjoyed, or choose a new one.

So much for strangers. If there's anything more difficult or scary than dealing with people we *don't* know, it's dealing with people we know intimately. In the next chapter you'll read about close relationships—particularly those with friends of the opposite sex—and how to survive even if the relationship doesn't.

9.
How's Your
Love Life?

Well, how is that love life of yours? Do you sometimes feel as though there isn't *any* love in your life? Hey—don't we all.

You have a good idea now why your life is the way it is, and you control more of it than you used to. But how does one control a love life? How do you get into a romantic relationship, assert your fifty-percent control of it, and still keep that "ol' black magic" going?

A good starting point is to remember that romantic relationships are *equal relationships*—whether you're a male or female—just like friends. Let that sink in.

Women, in the past, have been taught to *react* to things, rather than *act* upon a situation to change it. In romance, this meant that whatever happened in the relationship would depend on how the man thought things should go. Once he made that clear, the woman would be allowed to react to his decision, one way or the other. But in the end, his word was final.

Doesn't that sound boring?

It's a good thing times have changed, for both sexes.

When men had to make all of the decisions in a relationship, it just wasn't fair to either person. A man in his "proper role" had to be too strong to be human; he wasn't allowed to be gentle or show all of his feelings. He wasn't even allowed to assert all of his rights! A *"real* man" wasn't supposed to say, "I don't know," or "I don't understand." He was supposed to know and take care of everything.

Likewise, a woman had to be gentle and a little helpless *all* of the time, because that was her role. Even if she knew what to do in a certain situation, and didn't want (or need) to bother somebody for help, she had to wait until a man decided it was OK. She didn't have the right to judge her own actions, because there *were* no actions that were really her own. They all depended on men. And, unlike a man, a woman was *expected* to say, "I don't know," even if she knew better.

Surprisingly, there are still a lot of people who feel that way—even though, in these times when everyone is encouraged to do what works best for them, those people are a little embarrassed to admit it. Some people still decide what to do by saying, "I'll do *this* in this situation because that's what a man (or woman) is *supposed* to do." Meanwhile, the world around them is saying, "I'll do this because it's what will work best for me, for this relationship, and *it will be effective."*

Is it possible that you still carry some of that old, useless sex-role conditioning in the back of your head? Take this short quiz and find out. If you put a check mark (√) beside *any* of the following statements, you need to rethink your Rights and Skills. The great thing about assertiveness isn't only that you have certain Rights in your own life. It's just as important to realize that *every other person* has those same Rights. Keep that in mind as you read these statements.

_____ Girls—because they are girls—need to be taken care of sometimes.

_____ It's OK for women to have careers, but once they get married, all of that should end.

_____ It's wrong for a woman to make more money than her husband.

_____ Girls are more afraid of things than are boys.

_____ Boys are more brave and courageous than are girls.

_____ Boys are more independent than girls.

_____ Girls are more easily influenced by what people say or do than boys.

_____ Boys are better at making decisions than girls.

_____ It's better for girls to help with chores around the house and leave the outside work to boys.

_____ Girls are emotionally weaker than boys, who are tough.

_____ Girls are more easily hurt than boys.

If you checked any of the above as things you believe, spend a few minutes trying to figure out why. Is there any special reason why boys, for instance, are better at decision-making than girls? If they *were* better at it, it would mean that they should be *making* decisions, and that puts us right back where we were. Everyone would have an unfair burden. No one would have choices as to where they want to go or what they want to be.

Read the Rights and Skills chapter again. A romantic relationship has to be an equal one—in fact, it's not much different from having a very, very close friend. If that intimate *friendship* isn't a big part of the relationship, then there isn't much of a relationship to carry on.

GETTING CLOSER

So you meet someone you want to know better. You seem to have a lot in common, and you feel like your head's in the right place for handling some romance. It's spring—heaven forbid, you might even be falling in love! What happens next?

No one can move you closer to that person but *you*. Not even the other person can do it. You have to *follow through* with your feelings—ever hear of a solid romance in which the two people only saw each other once? It can't happen.

If you like someone and want to see more of him or her, do it. Find out what that person likes to do, and invite him or her to do it with you sometime. Of course, seeing someone often doesn't automatically lead to closeness. But you'll never know if you *can* be close uness you share each other's company a few times.

Whole books have been written on love and how to be successful at it. But if you have a crush on someone—or if you think your feelings go even deeper than that—you want to know how to get that relationship going *now*. Here are some ways to begin moving toward closeness:

1. If the other person doesn't know you yet, for heaven's sake, introduce yourself *now*. You already learned how to do that. If you think it will help, practice a few con- versation "openers" alone in your room first. Use the hints on starting conversations you read in chapter eight.

2. Follow up on your conversation. Suggest you see each other again (it's no sin to say, "I'd like to see you again"). It will be easier if you have a specific day and activity in mind; you'll feel more sure of yourself and what to say if you do.

3. Don't move too fast. Your first date is for exchanging information about each other, and finding out if you want to get to know each other better.

4. Don't work too hard at it. Concentrate, again, on *what*

you'll be doing, and things between the two of you will happen more naturally.

5. Follow your feelings—say and do what seems to feel "right."

6. Express your feelings. Be up-front about how you feel about the other person at *all* times, without being afraid of his or her reaction. If you're dying to say "I just love being with you" then say it!

7. Let the other person know that this relationship *means* something in your life. If you can't say that honestly— or if you're just going on with it because you don't have any other romance at the time—you shouldn't be in that relationship.

8. Don't feel as though you have to be included in every plan the other person makes, or assume that all of his or her free time "belongs to me." The best love relationships are the ones that don't interfere too much with other things you do, or other friendships.

9. In short, your love should be handled in the same way as you handle your friendships. You should be able to express all of your feelings and opinions, good and bad. When a problem comes between you, figure out exactly what it is that's bugging you, and *negotiate* a solution. Acceptance and honesty, adding up to respect, are as crucial with someone you're in love with as they are with your platonic friends. And your goal here, too, is to *BE A GOOD FRIEND!*

GETTING LAID WON'T GET YOU LOVED

Sooner or later, once you start getting involved with the opposite sex, the question of physical intimacy rears its not-so-ugly-but-plenty-dangerous head. But heads are a good place to start, so let's get into yours first.

Sex is a pretty confusing invention, whether you're a virgin (say "virgin" out loud; it's not a dirty word, no matter what your friends say) or have had a hundred sexual experiences.

What sorts of sexual fantasies (daydreams) do you have? Are they fairly tame, "cuddling" experiences? Do actual sex acts take place in your fantasies? Do things happen in them that other people would say are "weird" or even "kinky"?

Sexual thoughts are *normal,* no matter how "far out" you think yours might be. At times, you'll find that you will enjoy your sexual fantasy more than the real thing! That's fine—*any* sexual fantasy is perfectly all right, even if it's not about the person you're with at the time. Fantasies are healthy, and almost everyone has them—your teachers, your friends, and probably even your parents. If you sometimes feel guilty about your fantasies because they're too "dirty," or about someone you don't feel you should be thinking about in that way, end your guilt now. Go ahead and escape a little through your fantasies—that's exactly what they're for!

(Time Out: Write down your favorite sexual fantasy, if you have one, in your journal. Put everything down—where it happens, who is there, how you feel when it's happening. The next time you feel pressured and need a few minutes to escape, sit down and reread your fantasy. It will help.)

Another aspect of sex we're sometimes made to feel guilty about is masturbation. In spite of what you've heard, "playing with yourself" will *not* give you warts, cause you to go blind, or grow hair on the palms of your hands!

Masturbation is healthy and normal (but not necessary, so don't feel guilty or "left out" if you *don't* do it, either). Masturbation can help a person to explore his or her feelings and sensations—in other words, help a person learn "what feels good to me." Some people practice it when

they're feeling pressured, as sort of a relaxation exercise.
How often is too often to masturbate?

If you don't enjoy it, feel guilty about doing it, or just don't feel you're ready—*once* is too much. On the other hand, if you like to touch yourself, you're not a "bad person" if you do it every day. If you're a little scared of the idea, though, you're probably taking it too seriously to be quite ready for it. That's OK—*you* advance in your own good time to what feels good and right for you.

> (Another Time Out: Write your feelings about masturbation in your journal. What have you been taught by parents and other authority relationships about it? Do you agree with what you've been told? Have you ever done it? How did you feel, physically and emotionally, while you did it? How about afterward? Did you discover anything about your feelings and senses? Use what you write to help you sort out your feelings and attitudes about exploring yourself sexually.)

Now, things get *really* complicated.

You're in love, and your boyfriend or girl friend wants to have sex with you. You don't think you're ready for that part of your life to begin yet, but you're afraid that if you don't do it, your new love will make fun of you—or even leave you. What can you do?

These "myths" and "facts" should help you make up your mind.

MYTH: "You'll do it if you love me."

FACT: If your friend loves *you,* he or she will accept your limits. *You* have the right to be your own judge. If you don't want to have sex, and your friend insists that he or she can't have a relationship without it, express your feelings *specifically* and try to negotiate. No matter what, *don't* begin having sex unless *you* feel com-

have already reached its destination—the released egg—and it can be too late.

Of course, your decision about sexual activity will be based on your background and your circumstances—what your family has taught you, your age, your friends, and how important it is to you now. These thoughts about sex, though, are pretty generally accepted:

Sex is BORING when: (1) you're not *emotionally* intimate with your sexual partner first; (2) one of the people involved doesn't *really* want it; (3) one of the partners feels a little guilty about it; (4) it's done for "status"—so you can say you're getting laid—and not as a shared, loving experience; or (5) one person does it to prove he or she isn't inadequate.

Sex is OK when: (1) you're ready (not feeling guilty about it), even if that means waiting until you're married; (2) neither person goes around bragging about it; (3) both people are in love with each other; and (4) *both* partners share the responsibility of birth control.

AFTER IT'S OVER

These suggestions could have been included in the section on being alone. But nothing puts us down in the dumps like losing at love—or makes us more down on *ourselves.* So, if you ever get dumped (and you will—everyone does, it makes life more interesting, though it doesn't feel that way when it happens), read over the section on depression (chapter eight) to get yourself in the right frame of mind. Then, try one of these projects to get yourself out of the pits, feeling a little better, back in touch with the living, and maybe even learning something new!

1. Make a list of the twenty-five things you love most in the whole world. Keep it in your "special box," so you can look at it when you get the blues. (*Don't* put your lost love's name on the list—this is supposed to make you happy, remember?) Here's my list, to give you some ideas:

(1.) Harry Chapin's music, anytime.
(2.) The month of May.
(3.) Eating, unfortunately.
(4.) My family, each of them.
(5.) Leonard Cohen's poetry when I'm depressed.
(6.) My dog, Rasputin.
(7.) My electric pencil sharpener.
(8.) My Adidas.
(9.) Cuddling.
(10.) My wicker chair.
(11.) Hot, hot sun.
(12.) Cheese blintzes with sour cream.
(13.) My journal.
(14.) Strawberries.
(15.) Finishing good work.
(16.) Good and great friends.
(17.) Yellow roses.
(18.) Balalaika music.
(19.) Vermont.
(20.) My elephant collection.
(21.) Picking up the mail.
(22.) My front porch in the summer.
(23.) Chuckling to myself after I do something *very* assertive.
(24.) Reading *The Prophet* every year on my birthday, though I've come to disagree with parts of it.
(25.) Christmas trees.

2. Buy a big, bushy new plant for your room. Give it a name, and play some soft classical or jazz music to help it get accustomed to its new surroundings.

3. Talk to *one* person about the way you're feeling.
4. Run around the block. Don't return home until you've spoken to five dogs, children, or elderly people.
5. Pack a lunch in a paper bag. Take a bus downtown and, armed with a favorite book or magazine, eat your lunch in a park.
6. Renew a friendship you've let go for a long time; take the chance that the other person might not be all that thrilled to hear from you.
7. Make a family tree, listing at least five facts about each person. Where did they come from? How hard did they have it, and what feelings could they have had in their kinds of lives? How did they earn a living? Include past and present family in the "old country." Your parents should be able to help you out. Consider visiting relatives you've never met, after you graduate.
8. Have your handwriting analyzed.
9. With a notebook close to your bed, keep track of your dreams for one week. Then, find a "dream book" (you'll be able to find a number of them in the library) and look up the meanings of your dreams.
10. Have an emotional "estate" or "moving sale." The "possessions" you'll be getting rid of are your own characteristics, personality traits, or ways of behaving that you don't want to keep. Make a list of those. Beside each one, write a *better* trait or way of behaving that you *do* want to keep. When you're finished, hang the lists on your mirror, where you'll see them often, as a reminder.
11. Read *The Wall Street Journal* from cover to cover, and try to figure out why people all over the country read it every day.
12. Learn twenty new words and use them in the next week. You'll feel like a real intellectual.
13. Pick up your journal and read through your fantasies.
14. Listen to both sides of a favorite album you haven't

heard for a while. Don't do anything else while you're listening; just relax.

15. Buy a "racy" paperback and read the whole book in one evening.
16. Buy two concert tickets and treat an old, platonic friend to a night out.
17. Sleep in the nude for one week.
18. Take a piece of rope, two or three feet long. Sit alone in your room, with some music playing, and count the good things in your life—people or things that make you happy. For each one, make a knot in your rope. Don't stop until you have at least ten knots you're thankful for.

GUARANTEED HAPPINESS—YOUR OWN "TEN COMMANDMENTS"

Abraham Maslow, the famous psychologist, put down these ten rules for living in his book *Motivation and Personality.* If any list should be hung in a place where you'll see it every day, this one should. No matter who is pushing you around, making you sad, giving you pressure, or hurting your feelings—if you *truly* practice these ten commandments, every day, in all of your relationships, you will be able to sit back and say, "I don't have everything I want. But there *is* love in my life, and it is a good life that I have. I'm captain of my own ship—and, yes, I *am* a happy person." Take the helm—it really works.

1. Find humor in the human condition, not just in jokes.
2. Love others for being, not for what they can do for you.
3. Develop "clear eyes"—see the essence of things, and ask questions that get to the point.
4. Seek out new views of what is real, not new realities.
5. Try to consciously realize and enjoy your experiences.
6. Be comfortable in your own "home" (body).

7. Be unguarded; drop your awareness of your "audience" and know how *you* will feel after you do something, not how others will react.
8. Try to love things so much that you're willing to let them be what they are without your manipulation.
9. Refer to your own "inner Supreme Court" for judgments.
10. *Trust* yourself to be quietly and casually great, instead of having to show off and prove your greatness.

10.

Congratulations—You've Got Assertiveness! (Now, Use it.)

EVERYBODY AROUND YOU

You've probably already discovered that being effective isn't always easy. It would be if we lived in an assertive world—that is, if all the people we deal with respected our Rights and asserted their own. If we lived in that sort of give-and-take world, assertiveness would be a breeze.

Unfortunately, we don't. When you try to express affection to a friend of the same sex—even a little hug—don't be surprised if he or she backs away from you in embarrassment. If you're out with the crowd and you want to complain because the pizza you just picked up is stone cold, your friends might want you to just keep quiet about it, and not raise a stink.

By practicing *your* assertiveness Skills, though, you can help your friends and family to stand up for their Rights more often. You won't want to push them into being assertive (remember, each person is responsible for his or her own behavior). After all, if you want people to accept and respect your choices, you'll have to let them make their own, too.

The best way to spread assertiveness around is to *do it all the time. Practice* being an effective person—keep it in your mind every day, to do just that—and your family and friends will see that:

- *Being assertive isn't that hard at all.* It's just a matter of learning a new skill, and then using it every day.
- *It's the right thing to do.* Assertiveness is fair. you respect other people's rights, and they respect yours. Most importantly, *you like and respect yourself.*

If you're finding that your friends or family aren't accepting your new behavior very well, you may be doing something to make them uncomfortable. Being around an assertive person *should* help them to become happier and more free—free from old roles and phoniness with you, and free to make *their* own choices without worrying that they'll be judged by you. If it's not working out that way, this list of "Dos" and Don'ts" could give you a clue as to what's wrong.

Don't:

- Insult people because they don't assert their Rights. They just haven't learned the same Skills as you. If you have a suggestion for a friend who doesn't know how to be effective, begin it with a phrase such as, "You know what might work . . ." or, "I wonder if doing 'such and such' would solve the problem."
- Argue with people to assert your Rights—use your Clouding Skill instead.
- Let yourself get ripped off. Formal or commercial relationships are great for practicing Rights and Skills, because personal feelings don't get in the way as much as with friends. Be an *example* to your friends by *always* asserting your Rights in formal relationships—but don't preach about it. They'll see the results and want to act the same way.

● Get caught up in the "Queen Bee" (or "King of the Jungle") cycle. This happens when a person thinks he or she is a little superior to everyone else. Being effective does *not* make a person "better" than anyone else, it just *gets things done*, honestly, quickly, fairly, and with dignity.

Do:

● Ask for support from your friends and family. They'll accept your assertiveness if you welcome them into the process, instead of shutting them out. Ask them for honest criticism when they think you could have handled a situation more effectively. Ask them, too, to compliment you when they notice your asserting your Rights with Skills that work.

● When you get that kind of feedback, whether it's positive or negative, thank the person for caring. Take his or her comments seriously. Then evaluate the situation, and figure out if you agree.

● Give that same honest feedback to others, but take care not to put them down.

● Concentrate on giving *positive* comments whenever you can do it sincerely.

● Be flexible. Look for balance in your thoughts and actions.

START A RAP GROUP

One of the neatest ways to give and receive support (or honest criticism) for your behavior is through a "rap group." They're simply informal talk sessions, made of people your own age, for hashing out problems, talking over situations you're not sure how to handle, and sharing nice things that happen to you. They're fun and real learning experiences, and yield enough benefits to make them worth starting:

You're reminded of your basic rights. It's not that hard, when pressure sets in, to feel confused and forget which Rights you could be asserting—and which Skills you need to come to the rescue. The others in your rap group will help you sort it out.

You get emotional support and feedback. The group's criticisms could get a little harsh sometimes, but you never lose sight of the reason why you're all there: to talk about being more effective and to help each other reach that goal.

You get suggestions for changes. Sometimes we know a change must be made, but aren't sure just what would work best. A rap group will help you to figure it out.

You understand your own experiences better by talking about them with people who have pretty much the same experiences, and have handled them in different ways.

You can practice being supportive with others.

You'll share the joy—yours and everyone else's—as each of you conquers your hang-ups.

GETTING A GROUP STARTED

It's not difficult to get a rap group going. If you follow these easy steps, your group should be off to a good start!

1. First, spend a couple of weeks talking enthusiastically about assertiveness in general. Tell your friends how it has changed your life, and how much better you feel.
2. Invite six to ten friends to your house to begin your rap group. (With your parents' permission, of course.)
3. You take the responsibility for being "leader" the first night. Discuss why you're all there, situations in which

you have a hard time asserting yourselves, and topics the group might want to use as discussion "themes" on different nights.

4. Encourage each person to talk. Concentrate first on what you have in common, then branch out to different ways of handling the same situations.
5. At the end of your first rap session, the group should choose a new leader for the next session, *and* your "theme" topic for the next tune. That way, the leader will be able to zero in on his or her feelings on the subject.
6. Each session should have a new leader, so that everyone plays an equal role in the group.
7. Hold the session at a different person's house each time, and split the cost of pop or other refreshments equally.
8. Try to keep the size of the group at ten people or less, so that all of you can have your say. Two hours is a good length for rap groups. At your first meeting, set up a regular time, how you'll pay for refreshments, and how often you'll meet (twice a month is good).
9. All group members *must* agree that *everything* said in the rap sessions is *confidential.* Anyone who gossips to outsiders about what is said in the group should be given one more chance. The second time it happens, he or she should be asked to leave the group—the idea is to create a small community of trust and support, *not* to generate gossip. Each person has accepted the group's trust, and that shouldn't be abused.
10. Be *supportive* in other group members' efforts to become effective, and accept the same support from them. Be honest in your criticisms, but don't put anyone down.

GETTING HELP AND INFORMATION

Things go wrong for all of us sometimes—with our bodies, our heads, or at school—and we need to use the services of professional people. Here's how you can go about getting the help or information you need.

(It's best, of course, to go to your parents if you're in trouble or need to find something out. But there are times when that's just too embarrassing. If you feel you just can't take your problem to your family, or would just as soon not bother them with it, these are some of your alternatives.)

Medical Help

It usually makes sense, if you have a medical problem, to go to your family doctor first. If you're too embarrassed to see someone you know, or if you think the doctor might tell your family why you were there, or you don't even *have* a family doctor, look in your phone directory's yellow pages under "Clinics."

Many large cities now have "free clinics" that will examine you and treat you for a small donation—or, if you have no money at all, free of charge. You will find general health clinics, women's clinics (if you want information concerning birth control, or if you think you might be pregnant), and mental health clinics.

If you think you might have a venereal disease, you can call a free clinic—or, contact the National Free Clinics Council (1304 Haight Street, San Francisco, California 94117). They'll tell you where to find the one closest to your home.

If you do think you're pregnant, or need birth control information, your best bet is to call Planned Parenthood first. There are over three hundred Planned Parenthood centers in the country, and the office nearest you will be listed in the phone book. They will provide you with free counseling, refer you to a doctor if necessary, and it will be confidential. They will also examine you, if necessary, to determine whether you actually are pregnant. Many women's clinics (listed under "Clinics") provide the same services, but some will charge you for them. Ask which services are free before you set up an appointment.

If it's a specialist you need—for a serious skin or speech problem, for instance—ask your family doctor to recommend someone. If that doesn't work, look in the yellow pages under "Physicians & Surgeons Information Bureaus." You'll find a Doctors' Exchange, County Medical Society, or similar listings for referral services.

When you visit a doctor, remember that you have the same rights in *his* office as anywhere else. Assert them— ask a lot of questions. If he or she prescribes or gives you medicine, ask what's in it and what it will do. Also, when you're given a prescription, ask the doctor to put down the *generic* name, not a brand-name. The medicine will cost a lot less.

Don't let the doctor tell you that your questions or complaints aren't important. If he or she won't take the time to listen closely and answer all of your questions until you're satisfied, go to another doctor.

If you think you have a legitimate complaint about the way a doctor has treated you, put your complaint in writing. Explain exactly what happened and why you think it was wrong, and have your parents sign the letter. Send it to your local medical society (listed under " _____ (your county) _____ Medical Society"). If you receive no reply within two weeks, have your parents call the society and find out what's being done.

Psychological Help

Life confuses us all, and not knowing how to deal with our problems is nothing to be ashamed of. In fact, it's a sign of being a *stronger* person if you let a professional help you sort it out.

First, figure out what sort of help you might need. Is your problem a temporary one, and not too earth-shattering? If so, an appointment with your school counselor—or even talking to a friend who cares—might be all the solution you need.

If, however, your problem seems more serious—if things are really closing in on you, and you think you could use help over a longer period of time—there are other options.

Your school counselor, if you decide to go that route, will refer you to a public (free) clinic where a counselor will evaluate your problems and help you to learn what should be done to solve them. If there is a large university in your city, it may provide psychological testing and counseling through one of its clinics.

If you don't want *anyone* to know you're seeking help, look in the directory again under "Clinics." By law, all midsized and large cities must operate Community Mental Health Centers. These centers will give you free advice and counseling if you can't afford to pay—or, if you have a little money, charge you on the basis of what you can afford.

If you can't find a mental health center, ask at a free clinic or contact the National Clearinghouse for Mental Health Information, 5600 Fishers Lane, Rockville, Maryland 20852.

Legal Help

Minors (people under eighteen years of age) don't have many legal rights they can exercise without doing it through their parents. But if you feel you've been discriminated against, or your rights have been abused by a school, business, or other organization, have your family contact the local chapter of the American Civil Liberties Union (listed that way in the phone book). One of their attorneys will tell you if there are legal grounds for your complaint, and what, if anything, can be done. Their advice—and legal help, if they decide you have a case—is free of charge.

If you have questions concerning discrimination, employment rights, or women's rights, you can also contact the U.S. Civil Rights Commission, 1121 Vermont Avenue N.W., Washington, D.C. 20245.

What to Do if You:

● *Get an obscene phone call.* Hang up immediately, call the police, and then call the telephone company's business office. If it happens more than once, call the police and phone company again and they'll trace the next calls. Do NOT let the person keep talking (unless the police instruct you to do so, in order to complete the trace), act angry on the phone (that's what the creep wants), or let the caller know you're scared.

● *Are raped.* Call the police *immediately,* then call your local Rape Crisis Center. If the center isn't listed in the phone book, call the telephone operator and have her connect you. Call a close, supportive friend to be with you when the police ask you questions; the Rape Crisis Center will also send a sympathetic counselor to be with you. Make sure your parents are there. Do NOT take a bath or change your clothes; the police will need to make tests on you for evidence.

● *Think you're receiving unfair treatment at school.* Involve your parents in the complaint process. First, write down your complaints—what has been happening, who is involved, everything you can think of about the incident or problem—clearly and honestly. Present your complaint to your parents, who should set up an appointment with the school principal. If that fails to get satisfactory results, have your parents contact the local school board.

● *Want to be a volunteer.* If you want volunteer experience in a field that interests you, get in touch with local hospitals, museums, theaters, nursing homes, libraries, mental health centers, or Red Cross. Most will have some sort of volunteer program, and welcome your help. You can usually work from only a few hours a week to several days, at your convenience.

The National Park Service uses 3,500 young volunteers each summer. If there is a national park near your home, and you think you'd enjoy working outdoors, contact the Office of Information, National Park Service, U.S. Department of the Interior, Washington, D.C. 20240.

In addition, these addresses might help you to explore other interests:

Public Interest Research Group, 2000 P Street N.W., Washington, D.C. 20036. This student-run organization conducts research on consumer affairs; you probably know them as "Nader's Raiders."

Common Cause, 2030 M Street N.W., Washington, D.C. 20036. A citizens' lobby, Common Cause works to promote public interest in all levels of government. There is a membership fee, with special rates for students.

American Freedom from Hunger Foundation, 1100 17th Street N.W., Washington, D.C. 20006.

Two organizations geared to achieving and keeping a clean world: Environmental Action, 1346 Connecticut Avenue N.W., Room 731, Washington, D.C. 20036. Also, Friends of the Earth, 529 Commercial Street, San Francisco, California 94111.

Your local Better Business Bureau, listed in the phone book under that name. If you have a complaint about a store or business, or think you've been cheated, the B.B.B. will investigate your complaint.

Women in Apprenticeship, 593 Market Street, San

Francisco, California 94105, will help you out if you're female and hoping to enter a technical or nontraditionally female (like construction work, plumbing, or electrical work) profession.

Outdoor Sports and Travel

If you like being outdoors or love to travel, and think you'd enjoy doing it with other people your own age, contact these organizations for information:

American Camping Association, 342 Madison Avenue, New York, New York 10017. Ask for a list of camps, and tell them of your special interests.

National Campers and Hikers Association, 7172 Transit Road, Buffalo, New York 14221. They have local chapters and sponsor camping and hiking excursions for young people.

Sierra Club, 1050 Mills Tower, 220 Bush Street, San Francisco, California 94104. Sierra Club has local chapters and sponsors young people's excursions for camping, hiking, canoeing, river rafting, and horseback riding.

American Youth Hostel Trips, 132 Spring Street, New York, New York 10012. Sponsors bicycling trips for people fourteen years and older in the United States.

Outward Bound, Isaac Newton Square, Reston, Virginia 22070. Sponsors "survival schools" for people sixteen and a half years old or over; contact them for a list of the schools.

American Canoe Association, 1217 Spring Garden Street, Philadelphia, Pennsylvania 19123. Sponsors group canoeing trips. Also, American White Water Affiliation, 456 Hawthorne, San Bruno, California 94066.

If you want to go on a bus, bike, or sight-seeing trip, these organizations sponsor a variety of such tours for people under eighteen years of age:

American Youth Hostels, 20 West 17th Street, New York, New York 10111

Student International Travel Association (SITA), 50 Rockefeller Plaza, New York, New York 10020
Arista World Travel, 1 Rockefeller Plaza, New York, New York 10020

BOOKS FOR THE ASSERTIVE YOU

Do You Hate to Read?

Written by the National Council of Teachers of English, a dandy little book called *High Interest, Easy Reading* is for students who can read but hate to do it. If you just can't see the magic other people find in the written word, you're missing something. Send ninety-five cents to Scholastic Magazines, Inc., 50 West 44th Street, New York, New York 10036, and ask for the latest edition of the booklet.

Hooked on Assertiveness?

If you're pleased with the way your life is changing, now that you practice your Rights and Skills as a way of life, you might want to read more about being assertive. These books are recommended because they contain a lot of exercises you'll have fun with:

The Art of Hanging Loose in an Uptight World. Dr. Ken Olson. Greenwich, Conn.: Fawcett Publications, Inc., 1974. Many exercises; written for a slightly older group but easy to read.

The Seventeen Book of Answers to What Your Parents Don't Talk About and Your Best Friends Can't Tell You. Abigail Wood. New York: David McKay Company, Inc., 1972.

How to Decide: A Guide for Women. Nelle Tumlin Scholz, Judith Sosebee Prince, and Gordon Porter Miller. New York: College Entrance Examination Board, 1975. A paperback packed with self-exploring exercises.

You. Sol Gordon, with Roger Conant. New York: The

New York Times Book Co., 1975. Exercises on practically every page.

Woman's Almanac. Kathryn Paulsen and Ryan A. Kuhn, eds. New York: J. B. Lippincott Company, 1976. A great book, hodgepodge of articles and information on anything that would interest women today, and directory to almost everything everywhere.

Sex and Birth Control: A Guide for the Young. R. J. Liberman and E. Peck. New York: Thomas Y. Crowell, 1973. A detailed and straightforward discussion of contraception and sexual behavior.

Your Perfect Right. Robert E. Alberti and Michael L. Emmons. San Luis Obispo: Impact, 1970, 1974.

Our Bodies, Ourselves. Boston Women's Health Book Collective. New York: Simon and Schuster, 1973. This book, one of the most total and compassionate presentations of a woman's body and its functions, is practically a classic now.

I'm Running Away from Home but I'm Not Allowed to Cross the Street. Gabrielle Burton. Pittsburgh: Know, Inc., 1972. An easy-to-read, enlightening tale of liberation.

The Assertive Woman. Stanlee Phelps and Nancy Austin. San Luis Obispo: Impact, 1975. Lots of exercises, though many won't apply to women under eighteen, but worth picking up.

Free to Choose—Decision Making for Young Men. Joyce Slayton Mitchell. New York: Delacorte Press, 1976. Excellent guide to making decisions; sectioned according to subject or problem you're examining. Gives questions to ask yourself in making each decision.

A Bit of Insight

These books are easy to read and will give you a new perspective on some things that are happening around you:

A Hero Ain't Nothing but a Sandwich. A. Childress.

New York: Coward-McCann, 1973 Story of a thirteen-year-old heroin addict.

The Poetry of Rock. R. Goldstein. New York: Bantam Books, 1969. This book examines dozens of rock hits of the sixties, the effect of drugs through folk and rock, and each song's impact on American society.

The Loners: Short Stories about the Young and Alienated. L. M. Schulman, ed. New York: Macmillan, 1970. A collection of well-known short stories centering around the theme of alienation.

F.Y.I.

PsychoSources, A Psychology Resource Catalog. By editors of *Psychology Today.* New York: Bantam Books, 1973. Paperback collection of bits and pieces about the mind, how it works, and how it's been studied so far.

Youth Information Digest '74. Washington, D.C.: Workshops Press, 1974. Addresses of interest to young people, from Accuracy in Media (AIM) to Zoological Action Progress (ZAP). Some addresses could be outdated; check to see if a new edition has been released.

Classics and All That Jazz

Many students are surprised to learn that being stuffy or boring is *not* required for a book to become a classic. "Classic" means that, even though a book has been around for a long time, people are still reading it—because it's good! The ones on this list are dynamite, and great to curl up with. Most have been put out by several publishers, all are paperback, and a few more recent titles are included because they're pretty good and will keep being read, too.

TITLE	AUTHOR
The Bell Jar	Sylvia Plath
Cancer Ward	Alexander Solzhenitsyn
Five Smooth Stones	Ann Fairbairn
Of Mice and Men	John Steinbeck
The Grapes of Wrath	John Steinbeck
Buried Alive: The Biography of Janis Joplin	Myra Friedman
I Know Why the Caged Bird Sings	Maya Angelou
Silent Spring	Rachel Carson
Alice's Adventures in Wonderland	Lewis Carroll
The Pathfinder	James Fenimore Cooper
Great Expectations	Charles Dickens
A Tale of Two Cities	Charles Dickens
Siddhartha	Hermann Hesse
Brave New World	Aldous Huxley
A Separate Peace	John Knowles
Walden	Henry David Thoreau
Billy Budd	Herman Melville
The Glass Menagerie	Tennessee Williams